MICROCOMPUTING
IN
AGRICULTURE

MICROCOMPUTING
IN
AGRICULTURE

James Legacy

Tom Stitt

Fred Reneau

School of Agriculture
Southern Illinois University at Carbondale

Reston Publishing Company, Inc., Reston, Virginia
A Prentice-Hall Company

Library of Congress Cataloging in Publication Data

Legacy, James.
    Microcomputing in agriculture.

    Includes index.
        1. Agriculture—Data processing. 2. Farm management—
Data processing. 3. Microcomputers. I. Stitt, Tom.
II. Reneau, Fred. III. Title.
S494.5.D3L5 1984   630'.2'084   83–11200
ISBN 0–8359–4353–4

*Editorial/production supervision and
interior design by NORMA M. KARLIN*

© 1984 by
Reston Publishing Company, Inc.
A Prentice-Hall Company
Reston, Virginia 22090

10 9 8 7 6 5 4 3 2 1

Printed in the United States of America

*Dedicated to
the continuing advancement
of agribusiness*

Contents

Preface

Any study of the development of modern commercial agriculture must recognize the constant application of new and modified tools by farmers and ranchers. The microcomputer can be a powerful agricultural tool. Just as the producer who knows the principles of tractor operations is in a better position to make tractor-related decisions, so is the computer-literate agriculturalist better able to use the microcomputer.

This text will serve as a guide to both your hardware (computer machinery) and software (computer instructions) decisions. You may choose to have your computer needs custom designed by a programmer. However, just as many operations service, repair, and sometimes overhaul tractor equipment, you may decide to write programs that suit the individual needs of your business. In either case, an understanding of the computer's operation, including BASIC language and information that describes the function and purpose of microcomputer components, will enable you to make wise and profitable computer decisions.

A MESSAGE FOR FARMERS
AND RANCHERS

A complete microcomputer system can be purchased for under $500. Small businesses, corporate branch offices, schools, farmers, and ranchers are purchasing hundreds of thousands of these machines annually. The result has been more efficient and effective business decisions. Additionally, the role of the "personal computer" has been introduced. The home microcomputer plays, teaches, and records home management information. Our business and home life is dependent on computer operations that store and analyze information more quickly and cheaply than former methods.

The objective of this text is to illustrate effective and efficient applications of the microcomputer in agriculture. Sections One and Two explain jobs that the microcomputer can perform and identify the major parts of a microcomputer system. Section Three provides guidelines to enable the farmer or rancher to make microcomputer purchasing decisions.

Throughout this text continued reference will be made to the microcomputer as an agricultural machine or tool. In many ways, the microcomputer is to agriculture today what the tractor was to farming in the 1930s and 1940s. Computer applications on farms and ranches will enable producers to make better informed choices. Agricultural inputs of feed and fertilizers will be allocated in a more efficient and timely manner. The analytical speed of the computer will enable a dairy farmer to make individual feeding decisions for the herd of 200 milkers. Timely market information will be signaled instantly to the cash-grain producer as target price levels are reached at distant markets. Certainly, those farmers and ranchers who use the computer system effectively will have an advantage over those who either do not have a system or use systems with a lack of systems knowledge. Section Four is designed to provide this knowledge for the agricultural user.

TIPS FOR AGRICULTURAL
INSTRUCTORS

Each year in the United States in excess of 1 million youth and adults are enrolled in classes that study agriculture. These students are aware of a need to become computer literate. Many university, community college, and high school agricultural instructors have begun to incorporate microcomputer literacy into courses of instruction. This text is designed to be used as a primer for teaching an introductory course on microcomputer systems or as a supplemental reference for instructors who have added microcomputer applications to an existing subject matter class. This text will provide introductory subject matter for students enrolled in a microcomputer class and reference reading for those enrolled in other classes. Section Four is designed as core subject material for the microcomputer student and as a self-instruction guide for others. It is organized into 16 separate lessons designed to serve as self-instruction guides or as classroom assignments. Each lesson includes sample uses and example problems, with solutions provided in Appendix G.

MICROCOMPUTING IN AGRICULTURE

ONE

MICROCOMPUTERS AND AGRICULTURE

Computer History

In this chapter, an overview of the development of the computer, including recent microcomputer technology, is given. The microchip as a self-contained processing unit is reviewed.

Objectives

1. Review computer development.
2. Define a microcomputer.
3. Discuss how most people are already using digital electronics.

THE FIRST COMPUTERS

The first computer with digital capacity was constructed by the University of Pennsylvania in the mid 1940s. This early predecessor to today's microcomputer presented considerable problems for agricultural or home application. This first computer, called ENIAC, weighed some 30 tons and filled a room equivalent to slightly less than 40 feet by 40 feet. ENIAC used some 18,500 vacuum tubes and required about 130,000 watts of power to operate. The unit, because of its complexity and heat, could operate only a few minutes before tube failure. With all its limitations, it was the first digital computer to store ten-digit numbers and is the first generation of today's microcomputers.

The history of today's computer has been categorized into the following four eras or generations:

Vacuum tubes	Mid 1940s to mid 1950s
Solid state	1960s
Integrated circuits	1970s
Computer-on-a-chip	1975 to date

MICROPROCESSOR: THE COMPUTER ON A CHIP

Recent computer-on-a-chip technology has progressed rapidly largely due to the digital system. Originally, an analog system was used. A record player or a tape recorder is an example of the

Figure 1-1
Computer mainframe system: bulky and expensive.

Figure 1-2
Microcomputer: inexpensive and mobile.

analog system. The analog system records information using a continuously changing audio tone signal. Once recorded, the information is picked up by a receiving unit called a head or needle and sent to a large central computing unit. The electronically recorded signals produce an analogy for the sound signal, hence the name "analog." Linear circuits are needed to handle analogs. Some problems can still best be served by the analog system. However, the complexity of the analog system makes it unsuitable and inadequate for most home and small business uses.

The digital system is the most popular in use today and is primarily responsible for the progress in microcomputers. The digital system handles information in number form. The numbers can be altered to form letters, words, and many other symbols. The information system of a microprocessor is made up of a combination of units called bits. Bits are assigned a number of either 0 or 1.

Microprocessors are found in microcomputers (Figure 1-2). The microprocessor is composed of an integrated circuit that possesses the digital functions essential to be a central processing unit (CPU). The microprocessor that processes digital or number information can be combined or interfaced with devices like a television set, telephone, or printer. This combination provides for a transformation of digital information into video, sound, or printed information. A computer is called a single-chip micro-computer when all the functions of a digital computer are available in one integrated circuit.

Microcomputer science is a relatively new field in which new adaptations and applications of the processor are discovered almost daily. Tremendous commitments to research and development in this new and dynamic field are the reasons for such rapid change. The beginner is sometimes overwhelmed with the volume of information, technical facts, and complexity of terms and languages. However, advanced degrees are not required to be a user; in fact, most research in microcomputing is designed to result in a less complicated system. Today there are many conveniences that benefit from digital electronics in the form of microcomputers, computerlike controls, and/or microprocessors. A review may help to understand how most of us are already involved in the use of digital electronics.

The housewife who has a programmable microwave oven has already used a microprocessor. The digital electronic system allows the oven's operation to be predetermined or programmed to a specific set of tasks in a sequence determined by the operator. A program can set functions and time such as to defrost or cook at various temperatures for different periods of time. After one food is prepared, other tasks may be reorganized by the programmer (housewife) as desired for the next food to be cooked.

Calculators, once an expensive novelty, are now available for less than $10. Unlike the microcomputer, the calculator micro-processor (Figure 1-4) is designed for a specific and limited function. Most calculators are nonprogrammable, but still produce a computerlike function. The calculator provides the user a range of simple to advanced mathematics capability.

The programmable calculator is the next generation of the calculator. The difference is in the programmable use of a magnetic card memory or tape, which contains instructions to perform a predetermined task. The advantage is that the memory card can be removed and replaced. Hundreds of programs are available on cards and can be used to save hours of tedious labor to complete routine and repetitious computations.

Figure 1-3
Former tedious home tasks can now be more quickly accomplished by microcomponent cooking controls.

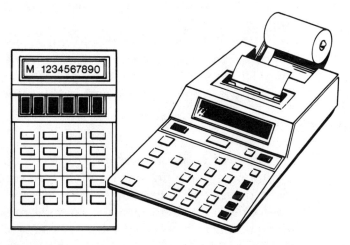

Figure 1-4
Calculators are inexpensive and can be programmed for many tasks.

Figure 1-5
Once popular family games may be replaced by computers.

Specialty and Novelty Uses of the Microprocessor

A computer-controlled camera employs a specially designed microcomputer that allows the operator to set the controls, much like a microwave oven, to achieve a desired outcome. The camera is automatically adjusted and focused in preparation to take a picture. This process allows for consistent-quality output from the camera.

Many of the electronic toys for home use and at arcades are controlled by computerlike devices, microprocessors, or computers. If the current trend is any indication, there will be more specialty uses of microprocessors in the future.

SUMMARY

The trend of computer technology from bulky and expensive mainframe systems to small and inexpensive microcomputers now provides a practical tool for the home and small business. The development of electronic toys, cameras, microwave ovens, and other computer-controlled items has made computer technology part of everyday life.

2

A Place on the Farm for Computers

Computer use in agriculture is relatively new. As microcomputers become economically and technically feasible for agriculturalists, microcomputing in agriculture will become a more common occurrence. Prepackaged programs, including access to specific agricultural information, are discussed in this chapter.

Objectives

1. Identify the factors associated with microcomputer use in agriculture.
2. Review ways microcomputers are becoming useful in agriculture and agri-related businesses.
3. Determine a need for microcomputer use in agriculture.

LIMITING FACTORS

The use of computers in agriculture has not been as dramatic as their use in large industry and business. The two major limiting factors have been cost and technical knowledge. The early generations of today's microcomputers were extremely expensive and featured components that restricted most agricultural applications. The agriculturalist could not afford to be involved in an unprofitable exercise. The cost of computers has dropped considerably and many units are within the limits of most production agriculture and agribusiness operations. Also, the technical knowledge needed to operate most microcomputer systems may be as near as your local high school or college.

GREEN THUMB

The introduction to computers for many people in agriculture and agri-related businesses has been through specialized prepackaged programs or software packages that can provide a service. An example is Project Green Thumb, which in Kentucky is serving selected farmers and business persons on a trial basis. The Green Thumb user can access the system through a keyboard identification number. The result is access to current (updated every 15

Figure 2-1
Nearby schools can provide computer training.

minutes) market prices, weather, news, and other agricultural information. Various configurations of this system are available in other U.S. farm communities. They can be operated using a microcomputer and an interface device in conjunction with a telephone and television. They require no knowledge of programming and can provide a valuable service to users.

A growing number of preprogrammed microcomputer instructions called software packages are available to the agriculturalist and do not require a knowledge of programming. Examples include the following:

1. Least cost ration
2. Fertilizer recommendations
3. Breeding records
4. Break-even analysis for vegetables
5. Milk production per cow

This list is only a brief example of the activities that a microcomputer can perform. Computer companies and colleges of agriculture have hundreds of agricultural packages available. New programs are being developed and constantly revised. The programs are designed so the agriculturalist can place or load a program's instructions into a computer's microprocessor. When a program is operated, it will request the operator to enter the data needed to complete a predetermined computation or other set of instructions. The data needed may be pounds of milk, cash expenses, pigs weaned per litter, current bank balance, or crop price information. These preprepared programs have been extremely beneficial in introducing the agriculturalist to the world of computers.

NEED FOR COMPUTERS IN AGRICULTURE

The need for computers for the agriculturalist is part of a continuing revolution in farm and ranch technology. When compared to other agricultural innovations, the microcomputer appears as the most recent new idea in the continuous pattern of efficiency generating agribusiness practices. In the early part of the twentieth century, a large proportion of the population was involved in production agriculture. As recently as 1940, approximately 34 percent of the U.S. working population were involved in farming. In 1980 less than 4 percent of the working population were employed on the farm. In 1980 there were 2 million farms. This is approximately the same number of farms there were 120 years ago in 1860. The peak in number was in 1940 with 6.5 million U.S. farms. The average size of a farm has increased from 150 acres in 1875 to approximately 480 acres in 1980. Of today's 2 million farms, it is reported that 20 percent of the farmers produce 80 percent of farm products. More of the agricultural products are produced by a smaller portion of the population.

At the same time that farm size has increased, so has the value of land. It has been estimated that the value of a corn-belt black soil farm in the 1940s was $100 per acre. The average 80-acre corn-belt farm was valued at $8000. In 1980 the average corn-belt farm size was 275 acres. In 1980 this black soil prairie land was valued at $3000 per acre. These factors, combined with equipment and buildings, gave the average 1980 corn-belt farm a value of nearly $1 million. Along with these tremendous increases in size and value came increases in production and in specialization of farm production.

The early agriculturalist was a diversified producer who entered into several enterprises to make efficient year-round use of inexpensive labor and costly equipment. In the last two decades, there has been an emphasis on specialization. The major rationale for specialization has been to produce one crop and to do so better than anyone else. Production per unit has been a factor in specialization. In 1900 the average U.S. wheat production was 12 bushels per acre. By 1980 U.S wheat yields were averaging 34.2 bushels per acre. United States corn production has an even more dramatic history, increasing from 28.1 bushels per acre in 1900 to 109.4 average bushels per acre in 1980. With increasing size and costs, the profit per unit of production becomes a most important factor to be planned for and achieved. Pigs marketed per sow, bushels per acre, pounds of marketed calf per cow, pounds of fruit and/or vegetable per unit (either tree or acre), pounds of milk per cow per pound of feed, tons of forage per unit of fertilizer, and eggs per bird are all specific facts that the specialized production agriculturalist now must know how to plan for and achieve.

The modern-day agriculturalist must have a way to manage the increasing volume of data to determine how to best use farm and ranch resources. Production per unit, whether it be pigs marketed per sow or bushels per acre, can be more easily increased when the production agriculturalist is able to manage each unit as a separate entity. The more efficient allocation of production resources to each unit of agricultural production is sufficient justification for farm and agribusiness consideration of computerization. There are, however, other factors.

Among other problems that confront the modern-day agriculturalist are tax considerations, labor records, alternative enterprise decisions, and decision within enterprises that are affected by weather, credit cost, market price, world price, world market demands, and labor and machinery cost. The microcomputer can be programmed to provide the user with specific answers that are based on alternative data as provided by the user. Lengthy mathematical problems can be completed quickly and redone several times for estimated future prices or situations. The production agriculturalist can then select the best alternative. As new information on prices and costs becomes available, the program can be rerun to establish an immediate estimate of the new information's impact. The computer can speed up the information calculation process and provide answers that lead to the selection of the most beneficial management decision.

The computer becomes a tool much like the tractor or the horse in times past. The microcomputer's ability to quickly calculate the anticipated result of alternative management decisions adds flexibility and timeliness to the farm or ranch manager's office.

SUMMARY

High cost and availability of computer education are factors that have limited the number of farms and ranches that use computer technology. In the past few years microcomputer prices have declined and computer education in agriculture has become more available. The microcomputer is now a viable tool for future farmers and ranchers.

3

Advantages and Uses of Computers on the Farm

The use of microcomputers in agricultural enterprises can save time and money. Time can be saved through quicker and more accurate record keeping. Money can be made through a more detailed analysis of the agriculture or agri-related business that leads to sound management decisions.

Objectives

1. Identify specific uses of microcomputers in agriculture.
2. Determine how the microcomputer system can be adapted to specific needs.
3. Create an awareness of microcomputers used to monitor agricultural activities.
4. Explain the use of computers in designing agricultural equipment.

THE TIRELESS MACHINE

Computers are promoted as a "cure-all" by some, a "wonder machine" by others. Computers cannot solve all the problems that agriculturalists of today and the future will face. The computer is a tool, and in order to make intelligent decisions about its place in modern agribusiness, it is important to understand what it can do.

Computers will complete routine and tedious tasks quickly, repeatedly, and without error. Accounting tasks that were originally accomplished manually, such as posting accounts payable and receivable, credit card and bank records, invoices, posting debits and credits in the accounting system, and inventory, can now be assigned to the computer. These time-consuming tasks can be delegated to the computer without fear of fatigue or error.

Computers can handle "volume number problems." The microcomputer has the capacity to handle a large volume of numbers quickly, easily, and without error. Problems that may require hours or weeks to achieve manually can be completed in a fraction of the time by a computer's microprocessor. Some agricultural-related problems are so integrated that changing one item like feed cost or expected production rates makes a determination of potential income at several price possibilities an untenable manual computation. These same tasks properly programmed are routine for the computer. Due to the management of information handled as bits, the computation can be achieved with a high degree of accuracy.

As production agriculturalists are required to make decisions on units within enterprises, the microprocessor's assets of speed and accuracy become important. Examples of this ability include the microprocessing ability to keep records for individual units of farm and ranch production. As detailed individual production information is provided, the microprocessor will store and analyze this information in accordance with previously programmed instructions.

For example, the dairy industry has known for decades that some cows within a herd may not be profitable. As herds grew larger, dairy animals were managed in groups. Each animal within a group received the average amount of feed needed by the group. Using this technique allowed one manager to care for more cattle. However, within each group some individual cows were overfed while others received too little feed.

With the speed and volume data capacity of the micro-processor, each individual of a 200-cow herd can be managed individually. The ability to handle the volume of data necessary to make individual decisions on a 200-cow dairy herd, 100,000-cage layer operation, or a 500-litter-per-year feeder pig operation is physically and financially possible with the assistance of the microcomputer.

Today's microcomputers are smaller, less expensive, and require less electrical power and less technology to operate than former systems. It has been projected that before 1990 most major computer companies will produce a briefcase-sized computer for $100 or less. Efforts are currently being launched by computer organizations to establish standard hardware, language, and software for microcomputers. This standardization, such as the use of BASIC language, will further reduce the technology required to operate a microcomputer. Once standardization is achieved, skills such as keyboard operations, basic language, and programming may be required school subjects.

Figure 3-1
Computer devices attached to livestock can monitor each animal's needs.

THE FLEXIBLE MACHINE

The ability to change a computer's instructions (program) and to link it to other devices, such as a printer, can expand the microcomputer's capacity and enable the accomplishment of greater tasks. Computer instructions or programs can be changed at the will of the programmer. The programmer by using a series of instructions can command the computer to analyze and report information in a variety of orders or sequences. The computer, through its microprocessor, will do exactly what was commanded and will continue until it is ordered to stop. If there is a need to change the procedure, order, or function of the instructions, changes are made in the program and not in the computer.

Thus a single computer can perform tens, hundreds, even thousands of tasks by simply changing programs. This greatly enhances the agribusiness value of the microcomputer. If additional tasks are desired beyond the capability of the basic computer, they can be achieved by the addition of appropriate components. Cassette tape storage or plastic disk storage of information and printing are functions that can be achieved by the addition of devices to the original computer machine. Knowledgeable computer experts are recommending that users such as agribusiness operators should identify the task to be completed, identify the software or program requirements essential to complete the task, and then secure the hardware that will perform the needed functions. Agribusiness professionals by the thousands need to achieve computer literacy if the maximum potential of microcomputers in agriculture is to be achieved.

FARM COMPUTER FUTURE

The future use of computers in the production of agricultural goods and equipment is expected to expand rapidly. Farm equipment has been fine-tuned, manufactured, and monitored by computers. This technology is most likely to gain wide acceptance and use in the decades ahead.

Monitoring Farm and Ranch Chores

It is difficult to imagine how computers will affect agribusiness by the year 2000, but we are able to see some interesting and exciting things even today. Microcomputers are currently being used to monitor irrigation requirements, thus saving production inputs and increasing production and profits. Microcomputers are available to monitor herbicide application and to measure and regulate the flow of anhydrous ammonia. Microcomputers are able to measure wheel slippage of crop planters and reduce ground speed to maintain seed placement distances.

Computer-Designed Agricultural Machinery

Computers are being utilized by industry to assist in the design of agricultural equipment. An example of this is a new industrial level computer system called CAD/CAM (Computer Aided Design/Computer Aided Manufacturing). Formerly, the manufacturing process had been tied to the ability of industry to transform what is visualized by the human eye into precise machine equipment tolerances. As equipment has become more complex, this link has been more difficult to achieve while continuing to produce a profitable machine. Experimentation with prototypes is time consuming and expensive. Illustrations of human tolerance errors in manufacturing circles are legendary (such as airplanes whose wheels do not have room to retract). Today, computer-guided lasers fabricate such items as closer fitting and more uniform fitting automobile doors.

The CAD terminal component can be programmed to display a composite of drawings, diagrams, or three-dimensional images of the components of a proposed machine. These modellike images are the result of equations and numbers that have been programmed into the computer. The speed of the computer allows for the proposed changes in the three-dimensional prototype to be displayed quickly on a television screen called a monitor. The impact of the change can be quickly evaluated and its interaction and impact on other components parts analyzed. Humans are visual animals and respond to pictures and lines much more rapidly than numbers and equations. The CAD component has allowed farm machine manufacturers to experiment with computer models of machines in a manner never possible with the physical object.

The design, test, and manufacturing process will be completed more efficiently and economically with computer assist-

Figure 3-2
A computer-aided farm machinery industry is providing quality equipment.

ance. Equipment that the future farmer and rancher uses may well be designed and manufactured by a computer system. This example is one of many that could have been used to illustrate the future use of computers in the field of agriculture. The full and total impact will be determined as new technology becomes available and is adapted to agriculture. The computer is a tool rapidly coming into the reach of every farmer and rancher.

SUMMARY

The microcomputer is a management tool that can be programmed to meet specific agricultural needs. While the microcomputer can be used to increase efficiency, it cannot take the place of sound management practices. Sound management must be employed in the selection of a microcomputer system that meets farm or ranch needs.

TWO

MICROCOMPUTER COMPONENTS

4

Introduction to the Microcomputer System

In this chapter we discuss the basic functions and devices of a microcomputer system. These functions include the input, processing, and output of information. The microcomputer keyboard, central processing unit, and the cathode-ray tube are examined. Then hardware devices and software components are discussed. The keyboard function is discussed along with an overview of the microprocessing chip. Software, an essential microcomputer component, is also defined.

Objectives

1. Identify the basic functions of a microcomputer system.
2. Determine the basic microcomputer devices used to input, process, and output information.
3. Identify microcomputer hardware components.
4. Define software.
5. Explain how the keyboard functions.

UNDERSTANDING INPUT, PROCESSING, AND OUTPUT

The microcomputer has many components. These components are grouped into two categories. The categories are termed (1) hardware and (2) software components.

The hardware and software components function with each other to perform the processing of data. Thus, the microcomputer processing system involves the input, processing, and output of data (Figure 4-1).

Raw information is fed into the processing system. The processing system converts the raw data into output processed information. The output processed information is provided to the microcomputer user.

INPUT, PROCESSING, AND OUTPUT DEVICES

Hardware is the equipment components that makes up a computer system. The microcomputer hardware basic components include an input device, a processing device, and an output device (Figure 4-2).

A keyboard is used to input raw information and instructions into the microcomputer system. The central processing unit (CPU) controls the operations of the microcomputer system. The cathode-ray tube (CRT) displays the processed information on a televisionlike screen.

HARDWARE AND SOFTWARE

There are peripheral hardware components in addition to the basic microcomputer system. Peripheral hardware is any device

Figure 4-1

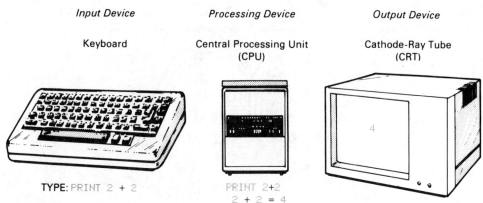

Input Device   *Processing Device*   *Output Device*

Keyboard   Central Processing Unit (CPU)   Cathode-Ray Tube (CRT)

TYPE: PRINT 2 + 2   PRINT 2+2   2 + 2 = 4

Figure 4-2

added to the basic input, processing, or output device to provide additional capabilities. The major peripheral devices for a microcomputer are the disk drive, printer, and cassette recorder.

The software component is necessary for the hardware equipment to function in the microcomputer. The microcomputer hardware is only as effective as the software, or programs, that operate a microcomputer system. Software is used to make the microcomputer system an efficient and effective data processor.

Software programs are "stored" on magnetic devices such as a plastic, recordlike disk or a cassette tape. When a software program is needed, it is copied from the storage device and entered in the microprocessor. The copied program is entered on a microcomputer chip.

The software programs are stored on a chip (Figure 4-3). The chip is a small, plasticlike device made of thin wafers of silicon; it forms the primary memory of the microcomputer. The chip is the place where information is stored and processed.

KEYBOARD

The keyboard terminal (Figure 4-4) is the device used to input data and to retrieve data. The keyboard is used to communicate with the central processing unit (CPU), which is located on the chip. The keys are arranged somewhat like that of a typewriter. Each key can command one or more specific functions, such as to record a

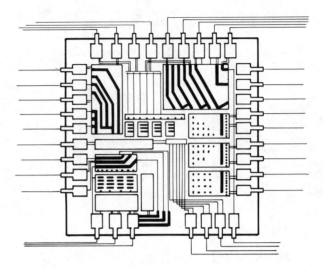

Figure 4-3
A computer chip one-quarter the size of your thumbnail.
A 64K chip can store 65,536 bits of information.

letter or numeral or to draw a figure. The manufacture of
keyboards is not standardized. Some manufacturers may stress the
graphics or drawing capability of the keyboard, while others
emphasize mathematic or word-processing activities.

Here's how a keyboard might work:

Step 1. Type this command: PRINT "HI JOE"

Step 2. Press ENTER (or RETURN): ENTER

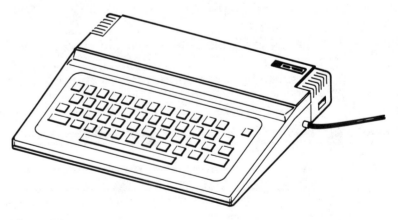

Figure 4-4
A keyboard is much like a typewriter.

The command to PRINT "HI JOE" was typed and entered into the memory of the central processing unit. "HI JOE" was displayed on a televisionlike screen as soon as the ENTER key was activated. In this case, the ENTER key signals the CPU to complete the set of commands that you typed.

SUMMARY

A microcomputer system includes the capacity to input, process, and output information. The basic microcomputer system includes a keyboard, central processing unit, and an output device.

The addition of a disk drive and printer or cassette recorder expands the capabilities of the basic microcomputer system. Software is used to operate microcomputer hardware. The keyboard is used to communicate instructions to operate hardware devices and software.

5

Microcomputer Systems Operation

The central processing unit and input/output devices, including the cathode-ray tube, printer, disk, and cassette recorder operation procedures are discussed. The information presented in this chapter will provide the microcomputer user with a better understanding of how a complete microcomputer system functions (see Figure 5-1).

Objectives

1. Explain the function of RAM and ROM in the central processing unit.
2. Identify the four major input/output devices.
3. Determine the difference between permanent and nonpermanent storage of information.
4. Review how each major input/output device functions.

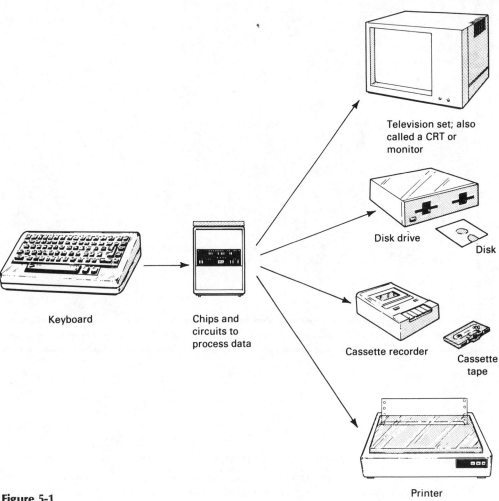

Television set; also called a CRT or monitor

Disk drive

Disk

Keyboard

Chips and circuits to process data

Cassette recorder

Cassette tape

Printer

Figure 5-1
Diagram of basic microcomputer system components.

CENTRAL PROCESSING UNIT: RAM AND ROM

The central processing unit (CPU) is the memory device of the microcomputer system (Figure 5-2). Information that is typed via keyboard is stored on a chip. The chip contains thousands of integrated circuits.

Basically, there are two types of memory. One is called random-access memory, or RAM for short. The second is called read-only memory, or ROM for short. RAM memory is storage space that can be used by the microcomputer operator to input new instructions or programs and to store data on a microcomputer chip. Information stored in RAM can be altered or erased. Turning off the power to the microcomputer will result in the loss of all information stored in RAM.

The read-only memory (ROM) also stores information onto a chip. The difference between ROM and RAM is that ROM is stored information that is not erased when the CPU is turned off. ROM usually contains stored information that is used over and over to operate the microcomputer. ROM can be changed only by rewriting the integrated circuits.

Here is how the central processing unit (CPU) works:

Step 1. The CPU (memory chip) receives raw information: 2 + 2

Step 2. The CPU transmits the processed information to an output device (i.e., CRT, printer, disk, etc.): 4

INPUT/OUTPUT DEVICES

Input/output devices allow the microcomputer operator to transfer information from or to the microcomputer system. The four major input/output devices are the following:

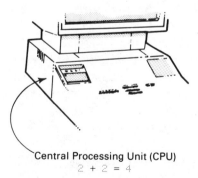

Central Processing Unit (CPU)
2 + 2 = 4

Figure 5-2
The central processing unit chip and circuits may be located with the keyboard.

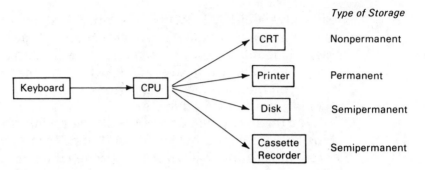

Figure 5-3
Three of four common storage devices offer permanent storage.

1. Cathode-ray tube (CRT)
2. Printer
3. Disk
4. Cassette recorder

Information that is stored in the microcomputers RAM will be lost once the CPU electrical power is turned off. The printer, disk, and cassette recorder can be used to expand the microcomputer memory and provide semipermanent storage of programs or instructions and recorded information (Figure 5-3). A printer provides a "hard copy" or paper storage capacity for the microcomputer.

CATHODE RAY TUBE OUTPUT

The cathode-ray tube (CRT) is a visual display device used to project information onto a televisionlike screen (Figure 5-4). The CRT provides video or visual display of the data entered into the keyboard terminal. The shortcoming of the CRT is that there is no permanent storage of data.

The cathode-ray tube (CRT) works as follows:

Step 1. The operator types a command.
Step 2. The typed command is transmitted to the CPU memory.
Step 3. RAM and ROM convert the information into a prescribed form.
Step 4. The typed information is displayed onto the CRT screen.

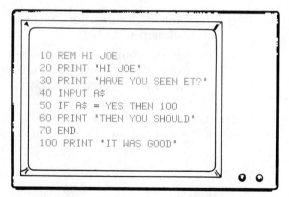

Figure 5-4
A television set is called a CRT or monitor.

PRINTER OUTPUT

The printer is an output device used to provide printed results of a product (Figure 5-5). The end product may be the results of a program or a listing of the program.

The printer works as follows:

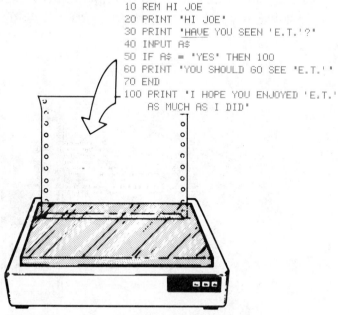

```
10 REM HI JOE
20 PRINT "HI JOE"
30 PRINT "HAVE YOU SEEN 'E.T.'?"
40 INPUT A$
50 IF A$ = "YES" THEN 100
60 PRINT "YOU SHOULD GO SEE 'E.T.'"
70 END
100 PRINT "I HOPE YOU ENJOYED 'E.T.'
      AS MUCH AS I DID"
```

Figure 5-5
A printer is used to produce a "hard" or paper copy of information.

Step 1. Transmit information to be recorded on paper from keyboard to CPU.

Step 2. Type the command used to open a printer's output line (see manufacturer's manual). For example, PRINT#-2:LLIST (TRS-80) or OPEN 4,4:CMD4:LIST (Commodore VIC-20) or PR#1 (Apple II Plus).

Step 3. Press ENTER (or RETURN).

Step 4. Printer records on paper the stored information.

DISK OUTPUT AND INPUT

The disk drive is the hardware or equipment used to access the diskette for saving output or retrieving input data. The floppy disk or diskette (Figure 5-6) is a magnetic device used to store data and programs. The disk device is an input and output device. Because of the speed and reliability of the diskette it is an excellent way to store data. Data can be transferred to a diskette at a rate of 500 to 1500 bits per second.

The following is an example of how one disk system works; check the operating manual of your system.

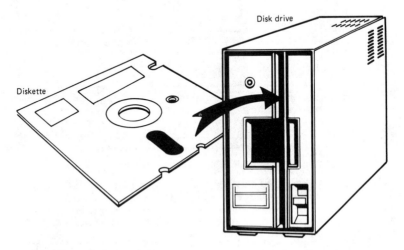

Figure 5-6
One 5¼-inch floppy or soft diskette can store more than 1 million bits of information.

Input: CPU to Diskette

Step 1. Originate program or data and transmit to CPU.

Step 2. Insert diskette into disk drive.

Step 3. Open communications line between CPU and DISK; that is, use substeps:

    a. Type SAVE "Program title" (Note: Open and save command varies by computer).

    b. Press ENTER (or RETURN). (Note: The data are recorded by a digital signal.)

    c. Once "READY" reappears to the CRT, the data have been stored.

Output: Diskette to CPU

Step 1. Insert diskette into disk drive.

Step 2. Open communications line between DISK and CPU; that is, use substeps:

    a. Type LOAD "Program Title" (Note: load command varies by microcomputer model).

    b. Press ENTER (or RETURN). Now the data stored on the magnetic diskette will be transmitted from diskette to CPU.

    c. Once "READY" reappears on the CRT, the data are available for use.

CASSETTE RECORDER

The cassette recorder (Figure 5-7) is the least expensive way to store data permanently. Audio tones are used to store the data on magnetic tape. The shortcomings of the cassette recorder in storing and retrieving data are the amount of time required to transmit data to and from the tape and the unreliability of the cassette tape after extensive use.

The cassette recorder works as follows:

Input: CPU to Cassette Tape

Step 1. Transmit program or data information to CPU.

Step 2. Insert cassette tape into recorder.

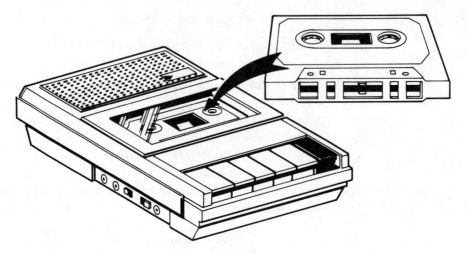

Figure 5-7
Cassette recorder and tape are an inexpensive storage alternative.

Step 3. Open communications line between CPU and cassette recorder. The substeps might be:

   a. Type SAVE "Program Title" (Note: Save command varies by microcomputer model).

   b. Press PLAY and RECORD on the cassette recorder.

   c. Press ENTER (or RETURN). (Note: The data are recorded by the frequency of the audio tones.)

   d. Once "READY" reappears on the CRT, the data are stored.

Output: Cassette to CPU

Step 1. Insert cassette tape into recorder.

Step 2. Open communications line between cassette tape and CPU; that is, use substeps:

   a. Type LOAD "Program Title" (Note: LOAD command varies by microcomputer brands).

   b. Press PLAY on the cassette recorder.

   c. Press ENTER (or RETURN) on the keyboard; the data stored on cassette tape will be transmitted from tape to CPU.

   d. Once "READY" reappears on the CRT, the data are available for use.

SUMMARY

The storage and processing of information in RAM and ROM are the key functions of the central processing unit. The non-permanent and permanent storage of information in input/output devices provides an efficient way to retrieve and reuse data.

THREE

SELECTING A MICROCOMPUTER

6

Making Dollars and Sense

The cost of a microcomputer system varies from a few hundred to several thousand dollars. Wise planning prior to the selection of a microcomputer system is essential in meeting the needs of an agribusiness.

Objectives

1. Develop an awareness that each agriculturalist must decide what microcomputer system is best for a given situation.
2. Determine items to consider in the selection of a microcomputer system.
3. Review the cost of various microcomputer systems.

MICROCOMPUTER PURCHASE
CONSIDERATIONS*

The use of microcomputers has expanded rapidly as their cost has decreased. Many small businesses and a few farms and ranches have been making computerized equipment decisions for the past ten or more years. The advantage that nonfarm businesses have that make them more adaptable to computerization is that many small businesses are exactly alike. A fast food or hardware chain store in California is very similar to one located in northwest Texas or southeastern Maine. This similarity has meant that one set of instructions could order goods or keep inventory for the chain store no matter where it was located. One program and one equipment setup could be determined to be the most effective and then easily placed in each chain store.

Farms and ranches typically have more business differences than similarities. The farm inventory may be a live plant or animal of a wide variety of species. Supplies needed by thousands of ranches on the eastern slope of the Rockies may never be needed by the citrus growers in central Florida. Each farm and ranch represents a different set of business practices and alternatives. What this means to you is that you, as the farmer or rancher, are in the best position to make the computer decisions for your agribusiness. There are, however, indicators that you can use to determine an appropriate computer decision. In this section we will list suggested activities that, when completed, will let you know whether or not to support the addition of a microcomputer to your business operation.

Before beginning to purchase microcomputer components or software, it is recommended that you do the following things:

1. Locate a computer store that specializes in business computers. Pick a computer game store only if you can keep your hands off the games. You can waste (but enjoy) a lot of valuable time trying and playing games with a salesperson. At this store, load up on literature available free or to borrow. Stay a short time, 30

---

*This chapter provides price information about microcomputers. The prices given are approximate 1983 prices. It is anticipated that future prices will decline as the supply of microcomputers increases.

minutes at most, and leave. Learn the prices and capabilities of the equipment and software available. Once you begin to understand what is available, repeat this procedure at a second and third computer store. This time ask about the computer services available. Again, stay a short while and retreat to learn by reading the materials you can borrow.

2. Now you should be ready to get your hands on a micro-computer. The best buy, if available, would be a short course at a nearby high school, university, or cooperative extension service workshop. Again, avoid a game or play demonstration work-shop. You will have learned by now that there are more opportunities to learn how to play microcomputer games than there are to learn business applications of the machine. While at the workshop, try as many short programs as possible. This will allow you to understand how many problems the micro-computer can help solve. Also during this class try to identify a local authority on agricultural applications of the micro-computer. It is likely that this person has already paid for the system learning errors that you may make.

3. Decide if you are going to purchase a business machine or buy a game machine. These are separate choices. An excellent game machine may be as inexpensive as $100. A poor business computer and a poor game machine may cost $300 or more. You can start a microcomputer system inexpensively if you know what your business needs are and if you know that the machine you are about to purchase can be expanded to meet these needs.

MAKE SOFTWARE CHOICES FIRST

When considering farm or ranch microcomputer business needs, determine the capability of available software or programs. Use the capability of the software description to determine which hardware specifications you will need. For example, if you want to balance rations for 100 dairy cows or more per month, a software dairy rations package must meet this requirement. A software package that will perform this task will include a description of the machine size and types of equipment needed. Even if you plan to learn to write your own programs, the software selection system is useful. Again, the software system of selecting the best micro-computer for your agribusiness means you will need to read the descriptions of agricultural software (see Figure 6-1 for an example).

The problem with this system is that not much agricultural software is available at the microcomputer store. The best source of agricultural software descriptions will be at a nearby agricultural junior college or university. You may also contact the high school vocational agriculture teacher or cooperative extension agent. Considerable growth is taking place in adding microcomputers to local school systems.

If you cannot find easy access to agricultural software, read the descriptions of business software that your local microcomputer dealer does have. You will find software that will do tasks such as prepare financial statements, record accounts payable, record accounts receivable, write payroll checks, keep inventory, order supplies, prepare correspondence with automated proofreading, and many more standard business chores. Reading the capabilities of these software items will give you an understanding of the appropriate system size needed to perform these tasks. Reading software descriptions will also let you know that in most microcomputer business systems the software will be more costly than the equipment. The software packages just listed may range in cost from $30 to $600 or more. Remember, learning

---

TITLE: Comparing Crop Alternatives

LANGUAGE: BASIC

MEMORY REQUIREMENTS: 42K Bytes

DISK SPACE NEEDED: 110K Bytes

PRINTER REQUIREMENTS: 80 Columns

PROGRAM DESCRIPTION

This program allows the user to enter a series of 14 possible crop costs, such as lime, fertilizer, rent, taxes, herbicides, and others. Crop income items such as cash sale or livestock value and plant residue values are added to determine the profitability of a planned crop. The program allows you to enter as many as five alternative crops and their expected costs and returns. The result is a chart showing potential profit or loss for each crop.

Program Availability: 5¼" Disk   Source: XYZ Ag College

Program Cost: $30

Figure 6-1
Sample agricultural software description.

about software is an important step in deciding which micro-computer to purchase.

MICROCOMPUTER SYSTEM LEVELS

Once you have determined the type of software that is appropriate for your agribusiness, look for the machine that will do the job most economically. Recognize that microcomputer hardware prices have been dropping rapidly. The reason for rapidly falling prices is that, as the great demand for micro-computers is beginning to be met, their price will more accurately reflect the cost of production. Estimates are that a 16K computer chip costs about $1 to manufacture and that the plastic keyboard costs less than $50 to make. Do not be surprised if today's $899 bargain is on sale next year for $499. This chapter will describe the approximate cost of three levels of microcomputer systems.

A Beginner's System: $100 to $875

The least expensive beginner's computer system is a small processor with a plastic pressure-sensitive keyboard. These microcomputers have a small memory, usually 4K or less, but perform the same binary processes as the largest microcomputer. They are usually not expandable or compatible with larger systems. The primary advantage is to provide you with an inexpensive experience with the operation of a microcomputer.

The pressure-sensitive keyboard (Figure 6-2) will connect to most black and white television sets. This will save the purchase of separate monitors. Most microcomputers have storage capability with the use of a cassette tape player.

Another type of beginner's system (Figure 6-3) is one that is inexpensive to start and can later be expanded into a standard farm or ranch microcomputer system (see Table 6-1). Such a system would include a $200 to $400 16K to 32K expandable beginner's computer with a portable black and white television set used as the CRT. A compatible $75 cassette recorder provides unlimited data storage, and a $300 printer accommodates printed output.

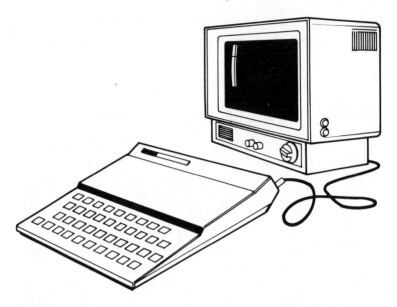

Figure 6-2
A pressure-sensitive keyboard is available for less than $100.

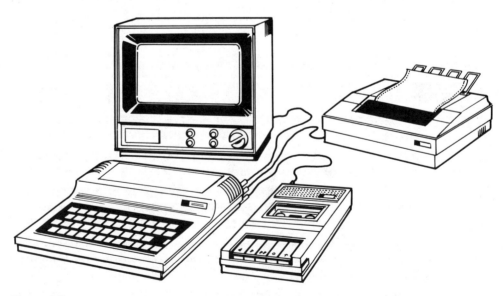

Figure 6-3
Low-cost but expandable microcomputers offer a good start.

Table 6-1
Beginner's Expandable System

	COST RANGE
16K to 32K expandable microcomputer	$200–400
Portable black and white TV used as monitor	$75–100
Compatible cassette recorder for unlimited storage	$50–75
Low-cost 80-line dot printer	$250–300
Total cost range	$575–875

A Standard Farm or Ranch
Microcomputer System: $2000 to $3600

Now that microcomputer prices have fallen, the knowledgeable consumer can purchase a lot of computer power in this price range for the standard system (Figure 6-4). Convenience and speed are the primary advantages of such systems. A 48K to 64K base microcomputer with a double disk drive can perform almost any farm or ranch computer task. Disk drives will store or retrieve data many times faster than cassette tape systems. The disk system

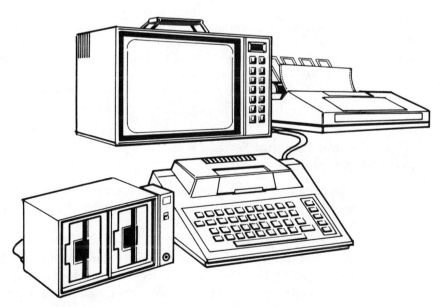

Figure 6-4
The standard system offers ease of operation and quick results.

also often provides a more detailed menu or index to each disk's stored contents. Selection of desired data or programs is almost immediate. Disk transfer rates range from 250K bits to 4500K bits per second. Both speed and convenience are the result of adding disk drives to a microcomputer system.

The standard systems printer is the user's choice. If farm or ranch to business contact using printed letters or information is essential, a better quality and faster printer may be necessary. The $800-range printers will double printing speed from 40 to 100 words per minute and offer improved letter quality and graphic capabilities. If these improvements are not necessary, the beginner's printer is quite satisfactory.

The standard system will include a high-resolution black and white CRT monitor. Monitors are specially designed to provide easy screen reading. This can be especially important if 30-minute or longer sessions of microcomputer use are being planned.

Table 6-2 provides a cost breakdown for the standard system.

Table 6-2
Standard Farm or Ranch Microcomputer System

ITEM	COST RANGE
48K to 64K microcomputers	$600–1200
Double 5¼-in. floppy disk drive	600–1200
Standard 15- to 17-in. black and white monitor	200–400
Standard 80-line printer	600–800
Total cost range	$2000–3600

An Expensive and Powerful System:
$4800 to $10,000 and up

The principal features of microcomputers within this price range are the addition of word processing and alternative computer language capability. The addition of a letter-quality printer is another added feature.

This system (Figure 6-5) is the ideal management tool for the farm or ranch business that involves hundreds of transactions daily and quality paper trail correspondence with suppliers and customers. The microcomputers within this price range will offer features such as COBOL and FORTRAN as standard languages and

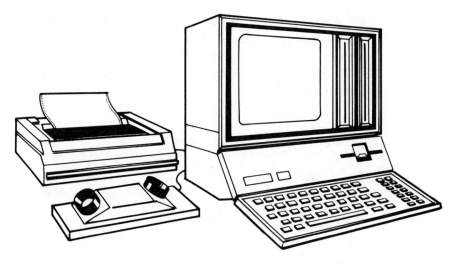

Figure 6-5
Professional-quality business communications from the farm.

the ability to program your own style of BASIC language with the use of a BASIC computer. Word-processing, letter-writing, and document storage and editing systems are easily added to this system. Such features as a 100,000 word dictionary software item can correct spelling errors and speed your correspondence.

A hard disk system may represent up to one-half of the cost of this system. However, for durability, speed, and accuracy, the hard disk is the best-performing storage system. A hard disk is composed of two 8-inch plastic disks that are permanently encased in a dust-free environment. With speed and accuracy, lengthy business analysis problems are dealt with efficiently.

A better quality interchangeable print wheel printer adds versatility and professional qualities to your business correspondence. Quality printers often feature 500 plus words per minute and "electric typewriter look" features.

The addition of a telephone-modem will link the farm or ranch office to market prices and the latest news or communicate with other microcomputer information centers. Several agricultural universities have expensive software systems available with a telephone link. The cost of connecting your system is usually reasonable and adds great programming capability to your system.

The graphic printer is useful when a visual or even a color display of graphics or charts is needed. Graphics are completed quickly and accurately with this option.

Table 6-3 provides a cost breakdown for the professional-quality system.

Table 6-3
An Expensive and Powerful System

ITEM	COST RANGE
48K to 128K microcomputers with word-processing capability	$ 600–2500
8-in. triple disk or hard disk drive	2300–5000
Standard 15- to 17-in. monitor	200–400
Letter-quality printer	1100–1800
Telephone-modem and graphic printer options	600–1800
Total cost range	$4300–11,500

SUMMARY

Systems are available from $100 to $14,000 and more. Certainly the best advice is for each farmer and rancher to invest some time in evaluating the microcomputer needs of the agribusiness before making a purchase. Remember that within the next five years, it is expected that nearly one million microcomputer units will become part of the American agriculture system.

7

Hardware and Software Options

The basic components of the microcomputer have been discussed in previous chapters. This chapter will address the extension possibilities of the microcomputer system. The extension of a basic microcomputer system allows the user to maximize and extend the capability of the microcomputer.

Objectives

1. Identify the hardware options and how each option works: modem, hard disk system, plotter, digitizer, and two-way information-retrieval system.
2. Identify software options and the function of each option: word processor, VisiCalc®, and information services.
3. Review software languages used in microcomputing.

Figure 7-1
A telephone modem connects your system to other microcomputers.

HARDWARE OPTIONS

Modem

The modem is a peripheral that will interface or connect the microcomputer to a telephone communication system (Figure 7-1). The binary signals from the microcomputer are converted into audio frequencies. Electronic signals are converted into high and low audio frequencies for telephone transmission. A microcomputer system that includes a modem option can send and receive information from other computers.

A modem, with proper software, can provide new sources of information. Informational systems such as the CompuServe Information Service and the Dow Jones News/Retrieval Service are accessible with a modem.

Hard Disk System

The hard disk system (Figure 7-2) expands the data storage capability of the microcomputer. Large amounts of data (5 million to 100 million characters of information) may be stored on a hard disk. Information is stored on platters, which can be permanently sealed in a dust-free environment. Hard disks are beneficial to the microcomputer user who finds that floppy disks are too slow or not large enough to store the needed information.

Plotter

The plotter (Figure 7-3) is a special printing device. A plotter can be used to create pictures, charts, or graphs. A software program must be used to link a plotter to a microcomputer's microprocessor.

Figure 7-2
The hard disk system is expensive but powerful.

Digitizer

The digitizer (Figure 7-4) allows the input of two-dimensional data into the microcomputer system. This peripheral is useful in such areas as architectural work and landscape design. This device can create a two-dimensional video picture of a designed building, machine, or other items. A graphics tablet is a peripheral used to create detailed illustrations. A graphics tablet software must be utilized with the peripheral. Pictorial information can be created electronically in displaying objects. For example, the graphics tablet could be a useful tool in the development of a landscape layout. The graphics tablet allows the user to create a paper copy of the designed item.

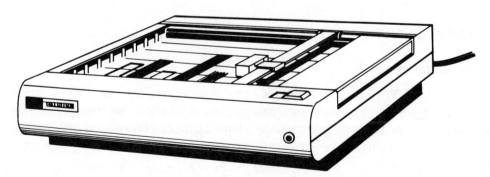

Figure 7-3
A plotter can draw charts or create maps and figures.

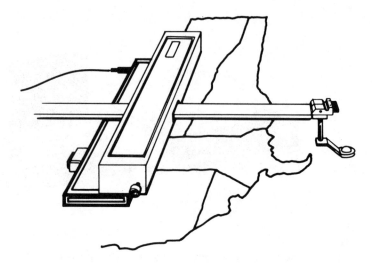

Figure 7-4
The digitizer adds a two-dimensional look to graphics.

Two-Way Information Retrieval Systems

Terminals are used to send and receive data. A telephone is connected to the terminal and antenna terminals are connected to a TV. Information concerning commodity futures, agricultural news, weather updates, and other data can be retrieved using this system (Figure 7-5).

The portable data terminal (Figure 7-6) allows access to a computer at any location where you have a telephone. Data can be transmitted or received while on the road.

SOFTWARE OPTIONS

Word Processor

Word processors are software programs for most microcomputer systems. Word-processing programs allow the microcomputer to accept and manipulate information as it is entered on a keyboard. Applications of word processing include letter writing, text revisions, and list alterations.

The word processor allows the operator to produce error-free documents. Also, characters and lines may be inserted or deleted from printed materials. Depending on the word-

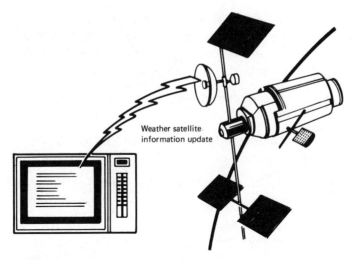

Figure 7-5
A two-way retrieval system can provide immediate access to new information.

Figure 7-6
A portable hook-up allows on-the-road computing power.

processing software purchased, the program may be able to do many other functions. These functions include but are not limited to hyphenation, scrolling, jumping, blocking, and formatting information:

  • **Hyphenation:** the capability to hyphenate words automatically.

  • **Scrolling:** the ability to move all information up, down, or side to side on a page.

  • **Jumping:** allows the operator to move to a specific page or line on a page.

  • **Blocking:** provides the user with a means to move a piece of information to be used in more than one location.

  • **Formatting:** the capability to alter how the information will be printed on paper or screen.

The capabilities of a word-processing package can be limited by the memory size of the microcomputer being used. First, the memory size must be sufficient to handle both the information being processed and the word-processing software. Forty-eight K of memory is usually considered the minimum size needed for completing word-processing tasks. Second, an 80-column screen, while not strictly required, certainly is recommended to maximize word-processing applications. Most major vendors of microcomputers can provide an 80-column screen at additional cost.

The selection of word-processing software should be taken seriously. Microcomputer memory, software memory requirements, and instructions to follow in using the software are critical considerations in the selection of word-processing software.

VisiCalc®

VisiCalc®, a management planning software, is organized in work-sheet forms by columns and rows. Once data are inserted onto the work sheet, any change leads to an automatic recalculation of all affected items.

The VisiCalc®, a product of VISICORP, Inc., is used as a part of the Minnesota Model Farm Business Analysis system. The F.A.R.M. (Farm Accounting and Records Management) is an accounting package that computes income and expenses for

Schedule F tax preparation. VisiCalc® is a worthwhile option to consider in developing a management system. Chapter 23 provides an introduction to spread sheet software such as VisiCalc®.

INFORMATION SERVICES

There is a growing number of computing services specifically designed for agriculture. Farmers, extension specialists, farm managers, and agribusiness people are interested in learning more about these agriculture information data-base services.

U/NO Agri-System offers a turnkey system complete with hardware and software designed for agriculture. This system features complete financial records, including balance sheet, cash flow, and income statements for each enterprise by month or year-to-date. The major limitation of the U/NO Agri-System is its expense.

AgriStar, an information service, can provide a range of information about agricultural commodity marketing, finance, news, production data, weather, and on-line time sharing of farm management models. This service is offered by Radio Shack with a modem-equipped Model II or Model III microcomputer.

Infoline is an agriculture computing information service available to subscribers of *Agricultural Computing Newsletter*. Infoline is designed to provide up-to-date information on agriculture and computer use. Once it has been established that you are a subscriber to the newsletter, you may acquire a password to access Infoline. Through a telephone and modem hookup, your microcomputer and terminal software can utilize the Infoline features. Infoline can be used with a variety of microcomputers.

TELPLAN

TELPLAN provides the sharing of computer technology and agricultural software programs. Software programs in agriculture are available to farmers, agribusiness, extension specialists, and others. The TELPLAN system uses the telephone to connect the microcomputer to the host computer. The service is available after an access number has been acquired from TELPLAN. The host computing center is located at the University of Michigan.

Software available from the University of Michigan may be accessible once a user ID and password have been established. A partial listing of available programs and approximate access fee is outlined in Figure 7-7.

FACTS: Fast Agricultural
Communications Terminal System

The FACTS network is used to link a terminal by telecommunications to the Ag Data Network at Purdue University. Terminals are located in county extension offices across the state of Indiana.

TELPLAN CHARGE RATES
UNIVERSITY USERS
EFFECTIVE JANUARY 5, 1982

Program Number	Description	Charge Fee	
		First Analysis	Adjusted Analysis
1	Compound Interest Model	2.30	.30
2	Investment Planning for New Dairy Systems	2.90	.60
3	Capital Investment Model	2.90	.60
4	Air-Blast Sprayer Calibration	2.30	.30
6	Apple Scab Spraying	2.30	.30
7	Spray Compatibility	2.30	.30
8	Weed Sprayer Calibration	2.30	.30
9	Plant Disease Identification	2.90	.30
11	General Linear Programming	2.90	.60
12	Swine Ration Formulation	3.50	.90
15	Poultry and Game Bird Ration Formulation	3.50	.90
17	Beef-Price Forecasting Model	2.30	.30
18	Crop Farm Planning Guide	4.60	2.30
19	Labor Estimator	2.30	.30
20	Livestock Feeding Planning Guide	3.50	.90
21	Livestock Farm Planning Guide	3.50	1.20
22	Corn Enterprise Planning Guide	3.50	1.20
23	Dairy Cow Cost/Return Model	2.30	.30
24	Swine Finishing Planning Guide	2.90	.60
25	Best Depreciation Method	2.30	.30
26	Best Ration and Feeder Type Selection Model	3.50	.90
28	Survivor's Income Protection	2.30	.50
30	Beef Cow Planning Guide	2.90	.60
31	Dairy Ration -R-	3.50	.90

Figure 7-7

Program Number	Description	Charge Fee	
		First Analysis	Adjusted Analysis
32	Amortized Loan Calculator	2.30	.30
33	Wet Corn Buying Guide	2.30	.30
34	Machinery Replacement Program	2.90	.60
35	Loan Refinance and Evaluation Model	2.30	.30
36	Financial Long-Range Whole-Farm Budgeting	2.90	.60
37	General Least-Cost Rations	2.90	.60
38	Silo Capacity/Cost Analysis	2.30	.60
39	Income Possibilities for Crops and Livestock	2.90	.60
40	Beef Expansion Cost Model	2.90	.60
41	Impact of Corn: Soybean Mix	2.30	.30
42	Dairy Pedigree Evaluation Model	2.30	.30
43	Machine Cost Calculator	2.30	.30
44	Beef Ration Formulation	3.50	.90
45	Heating and Ventilation Requirements for Cattle Shelters	2.30	.30
46	Michigan Dairy Farm Planner	2.90	.60
47	Calcium for Consumers	2.30	.30
48	Protein for Consumers	2.30	.30
49	Family Financial Planning	2.90	.60
50	Capital Investment Model	2.90	.60
51	Badger Ration Model	2.30	.30
52	Monthly Dairy Herd Growth	2.90	.60
53	Impact of Nitrogen on Corn Yields and Profits	2.30	.30
54	Life-Cycle Management of Swine	2.90	.60
55	Feeder Enterprise Planning Guide	2.30	.30
56	Simulation of Feedlot Performance of Gr. and Fin. Cattle	2.30	.30
57	Feedsheet Calculation for Beef Rations	2.30	.30
58	Batch and Crossflow Corn Dryers	2.30	.30
60	Dollar Watch	2.30	.30
62	Optimum Furniture Cutting Program	3.50	.90
63	Targets for Food Spending	2.30	.60
64	Data Expansion Program	1.20	.80
65	Dairy Farm Linear Programming	4.60	1.70
68	In the Bank or up the Chimney	2.30	.30
70	Crop Enterprise Cost Analysis	3.50	.90
72	Transitional Planning	2.90	.60
73	Dollar Stretcher—Budgeting for Unemployed Families	2.30	.30
74	Dollars and Decisions in the Supermarket	2.30	.30
79	Nutrition Spotcheck	.05	.02
80	Monthly Cash Flow and Resource Budgeting	2.90	.60
81	Budgeting for Retirement	2.90	.60
83	Heart Disease	2.30	.30
84	Alcohol Still Analysis	2.90	.60
85	House Hunter	2.30	.30
86	Stain Out	.50	.30

Quarterly Charge for Authorization Code   = $1.00
Quarterly Billing Charge for Project Account = $1.00

Figure 7-7   *(Continued)*

Software programs in agriculture are presently available through FACTS and new software is being developed.

AGNET: Agricultural Computer Network

AGNET is a computer linkage system located at the University of Nebraska at Lincoln. The AGNET system is an interactive computer system used in Nebraska, North Dakota, South Dakota, Wyoming, Kansas, Colorado, and Montana. Software programs are designed to provide the microcomputer user with relevant information.

SOFWARE LANGUAGES

The selection of a programming language must be considered in the development of a microcomputer system. The most frequently used microcomputer languages are listed and discussed next.

BASIC: Beginners All-Purpose Symbolic Instruction Code

BASIC is the most widely used programming language. Micro-computer users with little or no previous experience find BASIC a useful language. BASIC is a general-purpose, easy-to-learn language.

Pascal

Pascal is a programming language used on all types of computers. Pascal programming language is scientifically oriented and focuses on structured programming techniques. Some program-mers believe Pascal is a more useful language because it helps the programmer to write more reliable programs.

FORTRAN: Formula Translation

FORTRAN is a scientifically oriented programming language. To use the FORTRAN program, the problem must be defined step by step in specific statements. Since FORTRAN is applied to scientific as well as business problems, advanced mathematical operations are a part of the program.

COBOL: Common Business-Oriented Language

COBOL is designed for business and accounting applications. COBOL was developed to meet routine business needs and is written in an English-like language. Only basic mathematical calculations are included in COBOL.

SUMMARY

The capability of the microcomputer can be extended by the use of one or more advanced options. The modem opens new lines of information services for the microcomputer user. Software programs such as VisiCalc® and word processing widen the microcomputer's usefulness.

8

A Farm and Ranch
Sample Program

The ability of the microcomputer and microprocessor has been discussed from a general use approach. The questions still remain: What can the computer do for me? How can I apply it to my everyday tasks? How can it work for me and make money? Perhaps the best procedure is to preview a simple program that illustrates some of the capabilities of the microcomputer using BASIC language. This sample program was written for illustrative purpose and demonstrates only some of the ability of the microcomputer. The program is about depreciation.

Objectives

1. Identify the purposes and conditions of the Internal Revenue Service's Accelerated Cost Recovery System based on the Economic Recovery Tax Act of 1981 as set forth in the Department of the Treasury publication entitled "Instructions for Form 4562."

2. Calculate the dollar depreciation per year at any dollar input value for an item classified as a three-year, five-year, or ten-year property.

DEPRECIATION PROGRAM

The program is not complex but has some rather interesting features for the novice. To the experienced programmer, it may be considered quite simple. The program will be discussed line by line or by groups of lines. It is not the intent of this chapter that you should master all the commands used, but rather that you should gain an understanding of the overall concept.

Line 10 will not appear on the screen during program operations. It is a programming note to the user.

Line 40 has the program title with a time-delayed counter.

Line 50 has a clear screen command and formats the choice situation of lines 60 and 70.

Line 80, PRINT:PRINT, simply causes the computer to space a line.

Line 85 instructs the program to wait for your response.

Lines 90 and 95 instruct the computer to select either line 100 or 500 depending upon the INPUT.

Lines 100 through 450 provide a sequence of information about the Accelerated Cost Recovery System. There are PRINT: PRINT components to space for improved readability. FOR commands for time delays of various lengths are used to allow for reading and clear screen commands.

Lines 460 through 470 have a delay to allow the user reading comprehension time. The use of the STOP and CONT command places the time delay in the hands of the user and not the program.

If "B" was selected as an INPUT on line 85, the program would have automatically jumped to line 500. If "A" was selected, lines 100 through 470 would be executed prior to 500.

Lines 500 through 550 require the user to make a selection of alternative depreciation times. When the user selects an INPUT at line 550, the program will go to the appropriate line, 3000 or 5000 or 7000.

Series 3000, 5000, and 7000 operate essentially the same, with one major exception in 7000. Let us choose the 5000 series for illustrative purposes.

Lines 5000 through 5027 compute a depreciation schedule.

Line 5032 opens the lines to the printer (this command varies with each model and each company).

Lines 5035 and 5080 set up the chart and formulate the answer.

Line 5085 is the print command (this command also varies with each model and each company; check manual for correct command).

Lines 5090 through 5120 provide an opportunity to terminate the program or work another problem.

The 7000 series computes ten-year depreciation and differs from the 3000 and 5000 series at lines 7160 and 7170. Because ten years of information will not fit on a screen, lines 7160 through 7170 use the STOP/CONT command to hold the first five years on the screen for preview. Then the user commands CONT to move to years six through ten.

The depreciation program, shown in Figure 8-1, was designed to operate on a Commodore VIC-20 with a printer.

```
10 REM SAMPLE PROGRAM DEVELOPED11/20/82
40 PRINT"THE ACCELERATED COST RECOVERY SYSTEM.":FOR X=1TO4500:NEXT
50 PRINT"J":PRINT"THIS PROGRAM IS DESIGNED TO ALLOW YOU TO CHOOSE:"
60 PRINT:PRINT"---A. REVIEW THE CONCEPTS OF THE ACCELERATED COST RECOVERY SYSTEM
, OR"
70 PRINT:PRINT"---B. MOVE DIRECTLY TO DOLLAR INPUT VALUE FOR PROBLEM SOLUTION."
80 PRINT:PRINT"....PLEASE SELECT A OR B"
85 INPUT M$
90 IF M$="A" THEN 100
95 IF M$="B" THEN 500
100 PRINT:PRINT "THIS IS THE BEGINNING OF A DEPRECIATION PROGRAM EXPLANATION."
110 PRINT:PRINT"THE ECONOMIC RECOVERY TAX ACT OF 1981 CREATED A NEW METHOD OF DE
PRECIATION",
120 PRINT"THE NEW SYSTEM IS CALLED THE ACCELERATED COST RECOVERY SYSTEM"
130 PRINT:PRINT "   TIME DELAYED":FORX=1TO10000:NEXT:PRINT"J"
160 PRINT "YOU MUST USE THE NEW SYSTEM TO FIGURE DEPRECIATION FOR",
170 PRINT "MOST ASSETS YOU PLACE IN SERVICE AFTER DECEMBER 31, 1980"
180 PRINT"USE REVISED FORM 4562 FOR TAX YEAR ENDING AFTER DEC. 31, 1981"
190 PRINT:PRINT"   TIME DELAYED":FORX=1TO11000:NEXT:PRINT"J"
210 PRINT"IF YOU HAVE QUALIFYING PROPERTY YOU USE IN BUSINESS OR",
220 PRINT "HOLD FOR INCOME PRODUCTION, YOU ARE ALLOWED",
230 PRINT"TO DEDUCT A PART OF THE COST OF THE PROPERTY EACH YEAR."
240 PRINT:PRINT"THIS DEDUCTION IS CALLED DEPRECIATION."
250 PRINT:PRINT"   TIME DELAYED":FORX=1TO12000:NEXT:PRINT"J"
270 PRINT"DEPRECIATION BEGINS WHEN YOU PLACE THE PROPERTY IN SERVICE."
280 PRINT"IT ENDS WHEN YOU TAKE THE PROPERTY OUT OF SERVICE,OR",
290 PRINT"YOU HAVE RECOVERED ALL OF YOUR COST."
```

Figure 8-1
Depreciation Program

```
300 PRINT:PRINT"    TIME DELAYED":FORX=1TO6500:NEXT:PRINT"⊐"
330 PRINT " DEPRECIATION IS GROUPED IN TO FOUR CLASSIFICATIONS",
340 PRINT"THEY ARE AS FOLLOWS:"
350 PRINT:PRINT"    3-YEAR PROPERTY"
360 PRINT:PRINT"    5-YEAR PROPERTY"
370 PRINT:PRINT"    10-YEAR PROPERTY"
380 PRINT:PRINT"    15-YEAR PROPERTY"
390 PRINT:PRINT:PRINT "    TIME DELAYED":FORX=1TO4000:NEXT:PRINT"⊐"
430 PRINT"15 YEAR DEPRECIATION GOES BEYOND THE CAPABILITY OF THIS PROGRAM."
440 PRINT"FOR INFORMATION ON THE 15 YEAR DEPRECIATION REFER TO ";
450 PRINT"IRS PUBLICATION 534"
460 PRINT"WHEN YOU HAVE THE INFORMATION COPIED, TYPE CONT"
470 STOP
500 PRINT"YOU MAY SELECT THE DEPRECIATION SCHEDULE YOU WISH TO RUN BY ENTERING";
510 PRINT"THE NUMBER IN BRACKETS FROM THE LIST BELOW"
520 PRINT:PRINT"    (3) 3-YEAR DEPRECIATION"
530 PRINT:PRINT"    (5) 5-YEAR DEPRECIATION"
540 PRINT:PRINT"    (7) 10-YEAR DEPRECIATION"
550 INPUT N
560 IF N=3 THEN3000
570 IF N=5 THEN5000
580 IF N=7 THEN7000
2990 PRINT:PRINT:PRINT:PRINT
3000 PRINT "WHAT IS THE COST OR OTHER VALUE BASIS FOR THE THREE YEAR PROPERTY?"
3010 PRINT:PRINT:PRINT:INPUT A
3025 PRINT:PRINT"IF THE COST OF THE ITEM TO BE DEPRECIATED IS "A" DOLLARS",
3026 PRINT "THEN THE YEARS, PERCENT ALLOWED PER YEAR,",
3027 PRINT "AND THE DEPRECIATION IN DOLLARS PER YEAR WILL BE AS FOLLOWS:"
3028 PRINT:PRINT"TIME DELAYED":FORX=1TO6500:NEXT:PRINT"⊐"
3030 OPEN4,4:CMD4
3035 PRINT:PRINT" YEAR    PERC    DEPREC"
3040 PRINT:PRINT"  ONE     25    ".25*A
3050 PRINT:PRINT"  TWO     38    ".38*A
3060 PRINT:PRINT"  THREE   37    ".37*A
3065 PRINT#4:CLOSE4
3070 PRINT"DO YOU WISH TO SOLVE ANOTHER DEPRECIATION PROBLEM?";
3071 PRINT"PLEASE ANSWER YES OR NO":INPUT X$
3090 IF X$="YES"THEN50
3100 IF X$="NO" THEN 9000
5000 PRINT "WHAT IS THE COST OR OTHER VALUE BASIS FOR THE FIVE YEAR PROPERTY?"
5010 PRINT:PRINT:PRINT
5020 INPUT B
5025 PRINT:PRINT"IF THE COST OF THE ITEM TO BE DEPRECIATED IS "A" DOLLARS",
5026 PRINT "THEN THE YEARS, PERCENT ALLOWED PER YEAR",
5027 PRINT "AND THE DEPRECIATION IN DOLLARS PER YEAR WILL BE AS FOLLOWS:"
5028 PRINT:PRINT:PRINT"    TIME DELAYED"
5029 FOR X=1TO4500:NEXT
5030 PRINT"⊐"
5032 OPEN4,4:CMD4
5035 PRINT:PRINT " YEAR    PERC    DEPREC"
5040 PRINT:PRINT"  ONE     15    ".15*B
5050 PRINT:PRINT"  TWO     22    ".22*B
5060 PRINT:PRINT"  THREE   21    ".21*B
5070 PRINT:PRINT"  FOUR    21    ".21*B
5080 PRINT:PRINT"  FIVE    21    ".21*B
5085 PRINT#4:CLOSE4
```

Figure 8-1   *(Continued)*

```
5090 PRINT"DO YOU WISH TO SOLVE ANOTHER DEPRECIATION PROBLEM?";
5091 PRINT"PLEASE ANSWER YES OR NO"
5100 INPUT Y$
5110 IF Y$="YES" THEN 50
5120 IF Y$="NO" THEN 9000
7000 PRINT "WHAT IS THE COST OR OTHER VALUE BASIS FOR THE TEN YEAR PROPERTY?"
7010 PRINT:PRINT
7020 INPUT C
7030 PRINT:PRINT:PRINT"IF THE COST OF THE PROPERTY TO BE DEPRECIATED IS "C" DOLL
ARS,";
7040 PRINT"THEN THE YEARS,PERCENT ALLOWED PER YEAR",
7050 PRINT"AND THE DEPRECIATION IN DOLLARS PER YEAR WILL BE AS FOLLOWS:"
7060 PRINT:PRINT:PRINT"   TIME DELAYED"
7070 FOR X=1TO4600:NEXT
7080 PRINT"]"
7085 OPEN4,4:CMD4
7090 PRINT:PRINT" YEAR    PERC    DEPREC"
7100 PRINT"   ONE    8    ".08*C
7110 PRINT"   TWO    14    ".14*C
7120 PRINT"   THREE  12    ".12*C
7130 PRINT"   FOUR   10    ".10*C
7150 PRINT"   FIVE   10    ".10*C
7155 PRINT#4:CLOSE4
7160 PRINT"IF YOU WANT TO SEE YEARS 6-10 TYPE CONT  "
7170 STOP
7175 OPEN4,4:CMD4
7180 PRINT"   SIX    10    ".10*C
7190 PRINT"   SEVEN  9    ".09*C
7200 PRINT"   EIGHT  9    ".09*C
7210 PRINT"   NINE   9    ".09*C
7220 PRINT"   TEN    9    ".09*C
7225 PRINT#4:CLOSE4
7230 PRINT"DO YOU WISH TO SOLVE ANOTHER DEPRECIATION PROBLEM?"
7240 INPUT Y$
7250 IF Y$="YES"THEN 50
7260 IF Y$="NO" THEN 9000
9000 PRINT:PRINT"THEN THANK YOU, THE END":END
```

Figure 8-1 *(Continued)*

PROGRAM EXPLANATION

If you enter the Accelerated Cost Recovery System program in the computer and ask for a LIST, it should appear as in Figure 8-1. If you RUN the program and at line 550 you select (3) three-year depreciation and input $1000 at line 3010, you will get the following results:

YEAR	PERC	DEPREC
ONE	25	250
TWO	38	380
THREE	37	370

If at line 550 you select (5) five-year depreciation and input $1000 at line 5020, you will get the following results:

YEAR	PERC	DEPREC
ONE	15	150
TWO	22	220
THREE	21	210
FOUR	21	210
FIVE	21	210

If at line 550 you select (7) ten-year depreciation and input $1000 at line 7020, you will get the following results:

YEAR	PERC	DEPREC
ONE	8	80
TWO	14	140
THREE	12	120
FOUR	10	100
FIVE	10	100

When the operator types the CONT command, this will be the result:

SIX	10	100
SEVEN	9	90
EIGHT	9	90
NINE	9	90
TEN	9	90

Within each of three depreciation sequences, the user is provided an opportunity to "choose to solve another problem" or "END" the program.

As you review and use this program, you will have begun to understand the microcomputer's capabilities. The microcomputer can store information, receive information, and solve formulated problems. The program can contain a formula that can be used again and again to recompute new problems.

SUMMARY

The microcomputer is an excellent tool. It can be made responsive to your needs and desires. Like any other quality tool in the field of agriculture, the proper size of tool with the appropriate attachments in the hands of an experienced operator can be an efficient and profitable component of the agricultural operation.

FOUR

BASIC MICROCOMPUTING FOR AGRICULTURE

A FOUR-STEP APPROACH
TO BASIC LITERACY

Section Four is designed to provide self-instruction in computer literacy. Selected items of BASIC will be (1) explained, (2) demonstrated, (3) applied to an agricultural situation, and (4) tested for your ability to use. This introduction will define BASIC computer language and explain the purpose, content, and procedures of Chapters 9 through 23.

A Word about BASIC

BASIC is an acronym for Beginners All-Purpose Symbolic Instruction Code. It is an easy-to-use, multipurpose computer language. Following its development at Dartmouth College in 1963, it has become the most used computer language in the world. Nearly all microcomputers are built to work in BASIC language.

Complete the BASIC language in step 1 and your computer literacy will begin to show, probably enough to communicate with a local computer dealer or consultant. If you stick with it and complete steps 2 through 4, you will be on your way to writing or at least assisting in the design of your computer software needs.

Ideas for Using Section Four

Each computer command to be learned will appear in the small barn drawing at the beginning of each chapter. Commands will be defined and then explained with a series of questions and answers concerning the use of each BASIC language word or symbol.

Next you will be given general examples that require you to use each new command several times. Enter and practice each item several times. An effective practice procedure is to add to or slightly alter the use of the BASIC terms with your own ideas. Try several modifications, but only after succeeding with the book's example first.

Now the text will supply an agricultural application of the command. Again your ideas can be used here to develop computer use examples for agricultural situations. Finally, with each new command you will be given a self-test situation. You should try to complete this exercise on your own. A test sample solution for each text exercise can be found in Appendix G.

Caution: Be sure to enter or type in computer commands and programs exactly as they appear in this book. Remember, such easily confused symbols as the letter O and the symbol 0 are entirely different symbols to your computer.

9

Where to Start

The microcomputer can serve many functions. In this chapter we give the reader a general overview of where to start in the developmental process of BASIC programming. The PRINT statement as a mathematical and printed text function is discussed. The microcomputer's ENTER or RETURN is presented in this chapter.

Objectives

1. Turn on the microcomputer system.
2. PRINT math operations.
3. PRINT word operations.
4. ENTER or RETURN the PRINT command.

Where to start? A good question with a sensible answer. Follow the setup and turn-on instructions that are provided with your computer. Use the operation check procedures as directed by the manufacturer.

OK? or READY? This may be the same question your machine is asking you. Let's see if the machine really is ready.

Figure 9-1
The PRINT command instructs your machine to compute math problems; the PRINT " " command instructs the machine to print on the screen the message you place within the quotation marks.

Definitions

• PRINT: The PRINT command instructs the computer to print the message specified. The computer will print the message, messages, or expressions entered within the quote marks following the PRINT command. PRINT " "

• ENTER or RETURN: After the appropriate input has been entered, the ENTER or RETURN key must be pressed to instruct the machine to execute the command.

=========== **QUESTIONS AND ANSWERS** ===========

QUESTION   How can I get the computer to quickly add, subtract, multiply or divide?

ANSWER   Type the command PRINT; then add a number, add the math sign +, –, *, or / for division, and add a second number.

QUESTION   How do I tell the machine to go ahead and compute or print on the screen?

ANSWER	After typing in a PRINT command to compute a math problem, press the ENTER or RETURN key on the keyboard. This signals the machine to perform the command you have given.
QUESTION	Can the machine compute addition, subtraction, and multiplication or division in one command statement?
ANSWER	Yes; however, the machine will perform multiplication and division before doing any addition or subtraction.
QUESTION	Is there a means of getting the machine to add and subtract before multiplication and division are computed?
ANSWER	Yes; if the addition and subtraction is enclosed in parentheses (4+4)*2, the machine will add the 4+4 and then multiply 8 times 2 to compute the answer 16. Without the parentheses, 4+4*2, the machine will multiply 4 times 2 = 8, and then add 4 to compute the answer of 12.
QUESTION	Are commas and periods allowed when working problems?
ANSWER	Periods are allowed to be used as decimal points when working with numbers. Commas are not allowed and using them will result in a syntax error.
QUESTION	Will the computer repeat a word message with the PRINT command?
ANSWER	Yes, if you use the PRINT command and enclose the message to be repeated within quotations. PRINT " "

PRACTICE EXAMPLES

Try the following PRINT commands to compute math problems.

```
Command:   PRINT 7-4
           Press the  [ENTER]  or  [RETURN]  key

Result:    3
```
           The number 3 should appear on the screen
           directly below the command statement.

```
           PRINT 7-4
           3
```

Example 9-1

```
Command:   PRINT 42+63
           Press the  [ENTER]  or  [RETURN]  key

Result:    105
```
           The number 105 should appear on the
           screen directly below the command
           statement.

```
           PRINT 42+63
           105
```

Example 9-2

```
Command:   PRINT 16*4
           Press the  [ENTER]  or  [RETURN]  key

Result:    64
```
           The number 64 should appear on
           the screen directly below the command
           statement.

```
           PRINT 16*4
           64
```

Example 9-3

Command: PRINT 81/9
           Press the [ENTER] or [RETURN] key

Result: 9

The number 9 should appear on the
screen directly below the command
statement.

PRINT 81/9
9

Example 9-4

Command: PRINT 4+4*2
           Press the [ENTER] or [RETURN] key

Result: 12

The number 12 should appear on the
screen directly below the command
statement like this:

PRINT 4+4*2
12

The computer arrived at 12 by following
its rule of performing multiplication or
division prior to computing addition
or subtraction problems. If you had
wanted the addition to be completed
first, continue and complete the
next command.

Example 9-5

```
Command:   PRINT (4+4)*2
           Press the [ENTER]  or  [RETURN] key

Result:    16
```

The number 16 should appear on the screen directly below the command statement like this:

```
PRINT (4+4)*2
16
```

The computer will complete math operations within the parentheses prior to those not in parentheses.

Example 9-6

```
Command:   PRINT "COMPUTERS CAN HANDLE MATH QUICKLY"
           Press the [ENTER]  or  [RETURN] key

Result:    COMPUTERS CAN HANDLE MATH QUICKLY
```

The statement contained within the quotation marks should appear on the screen directly below the command statement:

```
PRINT "COMPUTERS CAN HANDLE MATH QUICKLY"
COMPUTERS CAN HANDLE MATH QUICKLY
```

Example 9-7

```
Command:   PRINT "FOUR PENCILS AT 19 CENTS EACH COST"4*19"CENTS"
```
Press the [ENTER] or [RETURN] key

```
Result:    FOUR PENCILS AT 19 CENTS EACH COST 76 CENTS
```

This statement in quotation marks
should appear on the screen directly
below the command statement. Notice
the math problem can be solved
within print statements.

```
PRINT "FOUR PENCILS AT 19 CENTS EACH
COST"4*19"CENTS"
FOUR PENCILS AT 19 CENTS EACH COST
76 CENTS
```

Example 9-8

AGRICULTURAL APPLICATIONS

Try the following problems.

```
Command:   PRINT "THE ACCELERATED DEPRECIATION OF A 5-YEAR 8,000 DOLLAR
           MACHINE IS"8000*.15"DOLLARS"
```
Press the [ENTER] or [RETURN] key

```
Result:    THE ACCELERATED DEPRECIATION OF A 5-YEAR 8,000 DOLLAR MACHINE
           IS 1200 DOLLARS
```

Remember the quotation marks must be around the statements
to be printed and not the numbers to be computed.

Example 9-9

Command: PRINT 'THE AVERAGE WEIGHT OF THREE HOGS WEIGHING
230 LBS, 218 LBS, AND 215 LBS IS'
(230+218+215)/3'LBS'

Press the [ENTER] or [RETURN] key

Result: THE AVERAGE WEIGHT OF THREE HOGS WEIGHING 230 LBS, 218 LBS,
AND 215 LBS IS 221 LBS

Remember the math rule is that all computations enclosed
within parentheses will be done first. Otherwise, multiplication
and division are computed prior to addition and subtraction.

Example 9-10

================ SELF-TEST EXAMPLES ================

1 Design a PRINT computation only statement that will
calculate the average production of four dairy cows. Cow 1
produced 12,000 pounds of milk, cow 2, 16,000 pounds,
cow 3, 11,000 pounds, and cow 4, 18,500 pounds.
Remember the order of the machine's math is to multiply
and divide before adding or subtracting.

2 Design a PRINT statement with the words to describe the
math result. The problem is to determine how many
pounds of nitrogen would be contained in 2,000 pounds
of fertilizer containing 33 percent nitrogen.

SUMMARY ══

The microcomputer user has learned to turn on the system and
use the PRINT command. Through the use of the ENTER or
RETURN key, the PRINT command is processed in the central
processing unit (CPU).

10

Write a Program

This chapter deals with how to write a simple program. The commands RUN, LIST, and NEW are discussed. The RUN command allows the user to execute a program. The LIST command allows the sequence of lines in a program to be displayed on the screen (CRT). The NEW command erases the random access memory (RAM) of all information. The new command has the same effect as turning off the (CPU).

The programmatic commands INPUT and A$ (A,A$, AB$) are also discussed in this chapter. These commands are used in the development of a sequence of instructions known as a program.

Objectives

1. Execute the RUN command.
2. LIST a sequence of instructions (program).

3. Erase a program from RAM with NEW.

4. Write a program using INPUT and A$ commands.

Now that you have mastered how to enter a one-line command, writing a program is next. A program is a series of numbered instructions that are not executed until all the instructions have been entered into the microcomputer's memory.

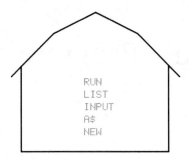

Figure 10-1
These commands, together with the PRINT command, are those necessary to write an interactive program. Interactive means you must add information to complete the program.

Definitions

• **RUN:** The RUN command causes the computer to execute the program. All variables entered in the program will be cleared when a run statement is executed. The computer will begin to run the program from the lowest numbered line. RUN 70 will start at line 70 and run the program from that line until the completion of the program or until you stop the program. If there is no line 70, a RUN may produce a UNDEF'D STATEMENT ERROR. Secure the correct line number and specify RUN.

• **LIST:** The LIST command allows the programmer to look at the lines that are currently in the computer's memory. LIST will list all the lines of the program that are in the computer's memory. If there are more than will appear on the screen, it will move to the end of the program. If the line needed is not present, it is possible to ask for a specific line (e.g., LIST 30). If more than one line is desired, it may be requested with LIST (the line number range desired), for example, LIST 10–40.

• **INPUT:** The INPUT command allows the person operating the program to put information into the computer.

• **A$:** The notation A$, or any letter followed by a $ when used in conjunction with an INPUT statement, signals the microprocessor to treat the received input as text. Any letter without a $ and used with INPUT causes the INPUT to be treated as numbers.

• **NEW:** The NEW command should be executed very carefully. This command erases the program and variables that are currently in the memory of the computer. This command is used when the user has finished with a program and has it properly stored on tape or disk or when the program is of no further value.

=========== **QUESTIONS AND ANSWERS** ===========

QUESTION   How does the microcomputer know which instruction line to perform first, second, third, etc.?

ANSWER   The microcomputer instruction lines are entered with a number title. The size of the number directs when it will be completed. The lowest numbered line is completed first and then each line in numerical order.

QUESTION   Why do program instruction line numbers typically appear as 10, 20, 30, etc., instead of 1, 2, 3, etc.?

ANSWER   The primary reason is to leave numbered spaces so that new lines may be added later. Use of instruction line number 10 and next 20 leaves nine empty spaces for additional instruction lines.

QUESTION   Can more than one command be put on one instruction line?

ANSWER   Yes, as long as each command is separated by a colon (:). Also, each instruction line is limited to a set number of characters. To make it easier to alter commands, most instruction lines of a program will contain one command.

QUESTION   Does each instruction line have to start with the cursor at the left?

ANSWER   Yes; in fact, you must press the ENTER or RETURN key after each instruction line is typed. If you do not, the microprocessor will ignore the second command you thought was entered.

QUESTION   How can I check a line entered to see if it is correct?

ANSWER   Any time you want to check a program that is in the microcomputer memory, clear the cursor to the left column by pressing the ENTER or RETURN key and enter the command LIST. Type LIST and enter the command by touching the ENTER or RETURN key.

QUESTION   Can I get the microcomputer to list a specific line or a set of specific lines of a program?

ANSWER   Yes, by typing the LIST command followed by the line(s) you want listed. Example: LIST 20 will list line 20; LIST 20–40 will list lines 20 through 40. On some machines the capacity of the LIST function may vary.

QUESTION   How does the INPUT command work?

ANSWER   The INPUT command causes the microprocessor to pause. The processor will wait until it receives new information from the keyboard or another input source. Once new data are added, the processor will continue the program.

QUESTION   Will the INPUT command cause the computer to receive any symbol?

ANSWER   Yes, if you let the microprocessor know what kind of symbol to expect. Use the A$ and A notation to notify the microprocessor what to expect.

QUESTION   How many characters can you use in a variable?

ANSWER   For most BASIC language versions, variables may consist of three characters. The first character must always be a letter. The second character can be either a letter or single-digit number. The third character, if used, must be either a % or $.

QUESTION   When must a % be used as the third character?

ANSWER   A % is used as the third character when the number to be inputted is to be handled as an integer.

QUESTION   What symbols does the INPUT A$ notation provide for?

ANSWER   The notation of INPUT A$, or B$ or A2$ for that matter, signals the microprocessor to treat the received input as text. This means any incoming information will be repeated when called for in any instruction lines.

QUESTION   What is text input?

ANSWER   Text input is contained within quotation marks " ". The microprocessor will simply repeat items placed in quotes; it does not matter if the items are letters or numbers. Numbers within a text input will not be computed. For example, numbers entered as "4+4" will simply be repeated in text as 4+4. Numbers entered as 4+4 without quotations will be repeated as the answer 8. In brief, the microprocessor will compute a listed number math problem unless you put it in text.

QUESTION   What symbols does the INPUT A notation provide for?

ANSWER   The notation of INPUT A, or C or X for that matter, signals the microprocessor to treat the received input as numbers. As so received, numbers can be added, subtracted, multiplied, or divided. This means that any computation entered under the notation A, C, or X as INPUT can later by repeated when called for in any instruction line.

QUESTION   How can data that have been entered under the INPUT command be recalled?

ANSWER   By entering the INPUT notation used to list the INPUT data in any instruction line after the INPUT has been entered. Example: INPUT X$ has been entered as a string or series of letters. Later in the program whenever an instruction line commands PRINT X$, the string or series of letters will be printed.

QUESTION   What do I do if I get a funny signal like ?? SN ERROR or ?? TM ERROR?

ANSWER   Usually errors detected are derived from an incorrectly entered instruction line. Refer to Appendix E to determine the error you have made. Then retype and reenter the line as corrected.

QUESTION   How does the command NEW work?

ANSWER   This command tells the microprocessor to remove the previously entered program from its memory. To save a program, place it on a cassette tape or a floppy disk. Read the next chapter for instructions on how to save a program. For now, before you begin a new program, remember to type NEW and enter the command by pressing the ENTER or RETURN key.

========================== PRACTICE EXAMPLES ==========================

Try the following examples as practice for writing short computer programs.

*If you are given an error message like ?SX?, retype the line exactly and enter.

Commands: 10 PRINT "MICROCOMPUTERS FOR AGRICULTURE"
            Press the [ENTER] or [RETURN] key

            20 PRINT "MAY INCREASE YOUR INCOME"
            Press the [ENTER] or [RETURN] key

            30 PRINT "WHAT IS YOUR NAME?"
            Press the [ENTER] or [RETURN] key

(New   40 INPUT A$
Command)   Press the [ENTER] or [RETURN] key

            50 PRINT "HELLO " A$
            Press the [ENTER] or [RETURN] key

(NEW   Type LIST and press the [ENTER] or [RETURN] key
Command)
                        The LIST command instructs the microprocessor
                        to print or repeat the program instructions on
                        the screen. Check each line to make sure
                        everything is in place.

(New   Type RUN and press the [ENTER] or [RETURN] key
Command)
                        The RUN command instructs the microprocessor
                        to operate or execute the program. The
                        microprocessor now follows exactly each of the
                        five commands listed on instruction lines 10, 20,
                        30, 40, and 50.

                        The computer should have printed lines
                        10, 20, and 30 as follows:

Result: MICROCOMPUTERS FOR AGRICULTURE
            MAY INCREASE YOUR INCOME.
            WHAT IS YOUR NAME?

                        At this point, which is line 40, you instructed
                        the processor to receive information or INPUT
                        from the keyboard. In fact, you said that input
                        in the form of text would be added here
                        (usually letters or words).

Example 10-1

Command: INPUT: type in your name or BILL and press the [ENTER] or
             [RETURN] key

                          Once this is done, the processor will
                          continue the program.

Result: HELLO BILL (or your name)

Example 10-1 *(Continued)*

Now let's continue by using the LIST command to add instruction lines to the program.

Command: LIST
              Press the [ENTER] **or** [RETURN] **key**

                          The processor will print the following
                          on the screen.

Result: 10 PRINT "MICROCOMPUTERS FOR AGRICULTURE"
              20 PRINT "MAY INCREASE YOUR INCOME"
              30 PRINT "WHAT IS YOUR NAME?"
              40 INPUT A$
              50 PRINT "HELLO "A$

Add: 12 PRINT "ANALYZE DATA AND STORE INFORMATION"
              16 PRINT "TO ENABLE YOU TO MAKE BETTER DECISIONS AND"

                          Remember to press the [ENTER] or
                          [RETURN] key after each instruction line.

              60 PRINT "THIS IS YOUR SECOND PROGRAM"
Command: LIST

                          Press the [ENTER] or [RETURN] key; the
                          result this time will be a "listing" of the old
                          program with three new lines.

Result: 10 PRINT "MICROCOMPUTERS FOR AGRICULTURE"
              12 PRINT "ANALYZE DATA AND STORE INFORMATION"
              16 PRINT "TO ENABLE YOU TO MAKE BETTER DECISIONS AND"
              20 PRINT "MAY INCREASE YOUR INCOME"
              30 PRINT "WHAT IS YOUR NAME?"
              40 INPUT A$
              50 PRINT "HELLO "A$
              60 PRINT "THIS IS YOUR SECOND PROGRAM"

Example 10-2

Command: RUN

> **Again be sure to press the** ENTER **or**
> RETURN **key**

Result: MICROCOMPUTERS IN AGRICULTURE
ANALYZE AND STORE INFORMATION
TO ENABLE YOU TO MAKE BETTER DECISIONS AND
MAY INCREASE YOUR INCOME
WHAT IS YOUR NAME?

> **The microprocessor is again waiting for text**
> **or letter input; use the keyboard to type in**
> **your name or** BILL **and enter. The program**
> **will continue to say:**

HELLO BILL **(or your entry)**
THIS IS YOUR SECOND PROGRAM

Example 10-2 *(Continued)*

From now on, this text will only occasionally refer to the
ENTER or RETURN key. Remember that to add an instruction line
to a program or to instruct the microprocessor the operator must
type in the appropriate command and press the ENTER or
RETURN key.

Command: LIST

Result: 10 PRINT "MICROCOMPUTERS FOR AGRICULTURE"
12 PRINT "ANALYZE DATA AND STORE INFORMATION"
16 PRINT "TO ENABLE YOU TO MAKE BETTER DECISIONS AND"
20 PRINT "MAY INCREASE YOUR INCOME"
30 PRINT "WHAT IS YOUR NAME?"
40 INPUT A$
50 PRINT "HELLO "A$
60 PRINT "THIS IS YOUR SECOND PROGRAM"

Add: 62 PRINT "WAIT UNTIL I SAY GOODBYE "A$
70 PRINT "SEE YOU LATER ",A$

> **Remember to use the** ENTER **or**
> RETURN **key.**

Command: RUN

Example 10-3

Result: MICROCOMPUTERS IN AGRICULTURE
           ANALYZE DATA AND STORE INFORMATION
           TO ENABLE YOU TO MAKE BETTER DECISIONS AND
           MAY INCREASE YOUR INCOME
           WHAT IS YOUR NAME?

Enter   BILL **(or your name)**
Input:

Result: HELLO BILL **(or your name)**
           THIS IS YOUR SECOND PROGRAM
           WAIT UNTIL I SAY GOODBYE BILL **(or your name)**
           SEE YOU LATER BILL **(or your name)**

                        You have now learned that the microprocessor
                        will continue to store and use the text stored
                        under the title A$ **whenever you call for it.**

Example 10-3   *(Continued)*

In order to remove a program from the microprocessor's memory, the command NEW can be used. A program may also be removed by turning the computer off. The NEW command works in the same fashion as LIST or RUN. Simply return the cursor to the left side by using the ENTER or RETURN key and type the letters NEW. Then enter the command by again pressing ENTER or RETURN key.

Command: NEW

                        Enter the command; nothing happened?
                        Try to LIST **the program you had in the processor.**

Result: OK **or** READY **signal**

Command: LIST

                        ENTER; **the result is another** OK **or**
                        READY **signal; this means the**
                        microprocessor's memory capacity no
                        longer has your program. You may now
                        add a new program. If you want the old
                        one back, it must be typed in again.
                        The next chapter will explain how to
                        save a program for later use.

Example 10-4

AGRICULTURAL APPLICATIONS

Here is an example that creates a table with agriculture facts.

First remove any remaining items from memory by using the NEW command.

```
Command:  10 PRINT "TOTAL AMERICAN CORN PRODUCTION"
          15 PRINT "IN MILLIONS OF BUSHELS"
          20 PRINT "YR/ACRE","TOTAL BU"
          30 PRINT "1900 - 28.1 BU",28.1*94
          40 PRINT "1949 - 28.4 BU",28.4*86
          50 PRINT "1960 - 54.7 BU",54.7*71
          60 PRINT "1980 - 109.4 BU",109.4*71
```

Note: the numbers 94, 86, 71, and 71 represent the number of millions of acres of corn planted in each year. The use of a comma (,) after the quotation marks will instruct the computer to divide the screen. It simply makes a better looking chart. Also notice that the numbers to be computed or multiplied are not in quotations. If you mistakenly place them in quotes, the processor will only repeat the numbers.

```
Result:   TOTAL AMERICAN CORN PRODUCTION
          IN MILLIONS OF BUSHELS
          YR/ACRE                TOTAL BU
          1900 - 28.1 BU           2641.4
          1940 - 28.4 BU           2442.4
          1960 - 54.7 BU           3883.7
          1980 - 109.4 BU          7767.4
```

You can use this format to create tables for your agribusiness. Later instructions will tell you how to get this table printed on paper (or, in computer language, on hard copy).

Example 10-5

The following example uses INPUT text and computation.

Command:
```
10 PRINT 'BUTTERFAT CALCULATION PROGRAM'
20 PRINT 'WHAT IS THE COW'S IDENTIFICATION NUMBER OR NAME?'
25 INPUT C$
29 PRINT 'WHAT IS THE COW'S MILK PRODUCTION?'
35 INPUT A
40 PRINT 'WHAT IS THE COW'S BUTTERFAT TEST?'
43 INPUT B
50 PRINT 'COW-'C$'-BUTTERFAT PRODUCTION IS,'A*B/100'-POUNDS.'
```

Result:
```
RUN
BUTTERFAT CALCULATION PROGRAM
WHAT IS THE COW'S IDENTIFICATION NUMBER OR NAME?
```

> The program will pause here waiting
> for a name; use X-2 or BOSSY.

Command: Type in and ENTER X-2; the program will continue by asking

```
WHAT IS THE COW'S MILK PRODUCTION?
```

> Again a pause; this time enter a
> typical annual production, say
> 16500 pounds.

Command: Type in the *number* only - 16500

```
WHAT IS THE COW'S BUTTERFAT TEST?
```

> Again a pause; enter a butterfat test
> number, say 4.1.

Command: Type in the *number* 4.1.
The program will complete its calculation and print on the screen the following:

```
COW-X-2-BUTTERFAT PRODUCTION IS, 676.5-POUNDS.
```

> In this program we used both a dash
> (-) and a comma (,) within the
> quotations to take up a letter space.
> Without these symbols the cow name
> would be crowded next to the
> adjacent letters.

Example 10-6

============================ **SELF-TEST EXAMPLES** ============================

1 Design a series of print statements that will present a
soybean production table similar to the corn production

table. The table should include three categories: the year, the yield per acre, and total production in millions of bushels.

YEAR	PER ACRE	TOTAL BU
1930	13.0	?
1960	23.4	?
1980	32.2	?

Remember, the use of a comma outside quotations will instruct the machine to divide the screen. In 1930, 0.9 million acres of soybeans were planted. In 1960, 24 million acres were planted, and in 1980, 71 million acres were planted.

2 Set up a series of one text input and two number input statements that calculates the daily weight gain of steer Joe-74 whose weight was 300 pounds when purchased and 975 pounds at market. There were 200 days between beginning weight and market time.

SUMMARY

In this chapter we discussed the commands used to execute a program (RUN), display a sequence of instructions (LIST), and erase a program from RAM (NEW). The programmatic commands INPUT and A$ were used in conjunction with the PRINT command to write a program. The final outcome of this chapter was the creation of the user's first program.

SAVE and LOAD

In this chapter you will learn how to store or SAVE computer information. As you have learned, microcomputer information is entered using the keyboard. You also know that information entered and stored on the microprocessor's RAM memory is erased whenever you turn off the microcomputer. This information can be saved or stored in several forms.

The two most convenient storage forms for most agricultural users are the mini disk and the electronic printer. Other storage devices include larger disks, hard disks, and cassette tapes.

Microcomputer information is most frequently stored on 5¼-inch soft plastic mini disks. This chapter will focus on how to store and retrieve information using the mini disk as well as on how to operate the microcomputer printer.

Objectives
1. Learn the SAVE storage command.
2. SAVE using a program title and device reference.

3. SAVE microcomputer information by printing a program.

4. LOAD information from the mini disk to the microcomputer RAM.

SAVE A PROGRAM

To SAVE a program is to DUMP the program. To DUMP the program means to transfer information from nonpermanent storage to a permanent storage device (e.g., cassette recorder, disk drive, or printer).

Figure 11-1
The SAVE command instructs the central processing unit (CPU) to transfer the stored program onto a storage device.

Definition

• **SAVE:** The SAVE command stores the program currently in the computer's memory on tape or disk.

Some computers use CSAVE in place of SAVE. The combination, options, and functions are the same. Check your operator's manual for the correct term. Some computers limit the number of letters in the program title.

The following SAVE routine is appropriate for VIC-20 Commodore machines only. Check your operating manual for your computer's SAVE procedure.

• **SAVE" ":** The SAVE" " command may be program-title specific. If you type: SAVE "BEEF FEEDING", the computer will save the program Beef Feeding and will store or file it under that title.

• **SAVE" ",8:** The SAVE" ",8 command is storage-device specific. SAVE "BEEF FEEDING",8 will store the Beef Feeding program on the disk.

• **SAVE,8:** The SAVE,8 command will store the first program on the computer disk.

If the storage device is not connected, the computer will say: DEVICE NOT PRESENT ERROR. When the SAVE command has been executed, the computer will return the cursor. Some computers will say READY.

QUESTIONS AND ANSWERS

QUESTION   What does it mean to SAVE a program?

ANSWER   To SAVE a program means to transfer information from CPU memory (RAM) to a permanent storage device.

QUESTION   What is a storage device?

ANSWER   A storage device is used to store programs or instructions permanently (e.g., cassette recorder, disk drive, or printer).

QUESTION   What should you do to SAVE a program?

ANSWER   Use the command SAVE by typing:
            SAVE *quotes program title quotes,* (a device reference number when needed); press RETURN.

QUESTION   Is the command SAVE the same for all micro-computers?

ANSWER   No! The command for saving a program from CPU to diskette for some commodore machines is:

OPEN 15,8,15

SAVE "title",8

To save on a TRS-80 disk drive, simply type SAVE "Title"

QUESTION	What does the command OPEN 15,8,15 do?
ANSWER	This command opens the line of communication between the CPU and the disk drive.
QUESTION	What does the comma 8 do?
ANSWER	The comma 8 tells the computer to save the program on a disk.

====== **PRACTICE EXAMPLES** ======

SAVE the following program.

Disk Drive

```
SAVE the program:
10 PRINT "MILES PER GALLON"
20 PRINT "HOW MANY GALLONS OF GAS DID YOU USE LAST WEEK?"
30 INPUT X
40 PRINT "HOW MANY MILES DID YOU DRIVE LAST WEEK?"
50 INPUT Y
60 A=Y/X
70 PRINT "YOUR MPG FOR LAST WEEK WAS" A
80 END

SAVE on diskette:
```

Turn on disk drive; insert diskette into disk drive.
(*Note:* notch in diskette must be on left side when
inserting diskette.) Type SAVE "MILES PER GALLON",8.
Once the cursor returns to CRT screen, the program is
on diskette. The 8 denotes disk drive on some machines.
Check manual.

Example 11-1

AGRICULTURAL EXAMPLE

SAVE this agricultural program.

Printer

```
SAVE the program:
 10 PRINT "AG ACRES"
 20 PRINT "HOW MANY ACRES OF CORN DO YOU GROW?"
 30 INPUT A
 40 PRINT "HOW MANY ACRES OF SOYBEANS DO YOU GROW?"
 50 INPUT B
 60 PRINT "HOW MANY ACRES ARE IN OTHER CROPS?"
 70 INPUT C
 80 D=A+B+C
 90 PRINT "YOUR TOTAL ACRES IN CROPS IS" D
100 END
```

To DUMP a program is to SAVE a program. To SAVE a program on printer, the command SAVE is executed in the following manner. Type:

> OPEN *file number comma command number colon* CMD
> *file number colon* LIST **press** RETURN

The program located in RAM will be printed out on paper. The command OPEN opens a line to the printer. The file number can be any number from 4 to 225 and is the same number used after the CMD command. The CMD command changes the normal output device from CRT to printer. Once the printer has printed the program, type PRINT #4: CLOSE 4. CLOSE 4 is the command to close the file. 4 is the file number. Some machines use the command

```
PRINT #-2
LLIST
```

Check manual for correct command.

Example 11-2

===================== **SELF-TEST EXAMPLES** =====================

1 SAVE the following program on a disk.

```
10 PRINT "AGE"
20 PRINT "HOW OLD ARE YOU?"
30 INPUT A
40 REM A=AGE IN YEARS
50 X=A*12
60 PRINT "YOUR AGE IN MONTHS IS"X
70 PRINT "THAT'S NOT SO OLD!"
80 END
```

2 SAVE the same program on hard copy (printer).

LOAD A PROGRAM

To LOAD a program means to transfer a program or list of instructions from a storage unit to the microcomputer's memory.

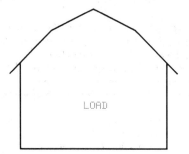

Figure 11-2
The LOAD command instructs the INPUT/ OUTPUT device to transfer the stored program into the CPU memory.

Definition

• **LOAD" "**: The LOAD command may use a program title: LOAD "BEEF FEEDING"

• **LOAD:** The load command transfers the program from the storage unit (usually a tape or disk) into the computer's memory for use or modification. The LOAD statement may be just the single word LOAD or CLOAD (for cassette tape).

• **LOAD" ",8:** The LOAD,8 command instructs the computer to search the disk for the program title in quotation marks.

• **LOAD,8:** The LOAD,8 command instructs the computer to load the first program on the disk.

QUESTIONS AND ANSWERS

QUESTION   What devices can be used in the storage of information?

ANSWER   The major devices include disk drive and printer.

QUESTION   How can I transfer information (instructions or program) from a storage device into the CPU memory (RAM)?

ANSWER   Type the command LOAD; then quotes, program title, followed by quotes; then press ENTER or RETURN.

QUESTION   Is the sequence of executing the LOAD command the same for all microcomputers?

ANSWER   No, the sequence for LOAD on some Commodore models is
             OPEN 15,8,15
             LOAD "title",8
             The command for the TRS-80 disk drive is
             LOAD"title"
             The command for the Apple II is
             LOAD (followed by the program title)

QUESTION   What does the command OPEN 15,8,15 do?

ANSWER   This command opens the line of communication between the CPU and the disk drive so that information on the disk is transferred into the CPU memory.

QUESTION   What does the comma 8 do?

ANSWER   The comma 8 tells the computer to search for the
                program on the disk drive.

================= **PRACTICE EXAMPLES** =================

LOAD the following example program into the CPU memory.
(*Note:* You must type and SAVE the program before you can
LOAD the program.)

LOAD **the program:**

```
        10 PRINT "MICROCOMPUTERS IN AGRICULTURE"
        20 PRINT "MAY INCREASE YOUR INCOME"
        30 PRINT "WHAT IS YOUR NAME?"
        40 INPUT A$
        50 PRINT "HELLO "A$
```

Type LOAD "MICROCOMPUTERS IN AGRICULTURE" **and press** ENTER
or RETURN **key. The** LOAD **command transfers the program to CPU
memory. Once the computer prints** OK **and** READY, **the program
is loaded into the CPU memory. Now you are ready to use the
program that has been transferred to RAM.**

Type and SAVE **a second program on your disk.**

Before LOAD**ing a second program, it is best to remove the first program
from RAM by using the** NEW **command.**

Example 11-3

Disk drive operating procedures:

        Turn on disk drive; insert diskettes into disk drive.
        (*NOTE:* Follow manufacturer's instructions when
        inserting diskette.) Type LOAD instructions. Once
        the cursor returns to CRT screen, the program is in
        CPU memory (RAM). The program is ready for use.

Example 11-4

```
LOAD the program:

    10 PRINT "BREEDS"
    20 PRINT "WHAT BREED OF DAIRY CATTLE IS THE BEST PRODUCER
       OF BUTTERFAT?"
    30 INPUT A$
    40 PRINT "WHY DID YOU SAY "A$
    50 INPUT B$
    55 PRINT B$
    60 PRINT "THANKS FOR THE INFORMATION."
```

Example 11-5

The disk and printer provide a greatly increased storage capacity for a microcomputer. The operating manual of each individual machine will provide the details of how to establish an index or directory to programs or data files that are kept on a disk. Care should be given to provide a clean storage place for disks. Magnetically charged dust particles are the most frequent source of printer and disk drive operating problems. Most manufacturers will provide cases or coverings to protect printers and stored disks.

===================== SELF-TEST EXAMPLES =====================

LOAD the following programs from a disk.

1 Title = Alfalfa

```
10 PRINT "ALFALFA"
20 PRINT "THIS PROGRAM WILL HELP YOU"
30 PRINT "FIND MORE INFORMATION ABOUT ALFALFA."
40 PRINT "DO YOU WANT TO CONTINUE('YES' OR 'NO')?"
50 INPUT A$
60 IF A$="NO" THEN PRINT "SORRY YOU FEEL THAT WAY.":END
70 PRINT "GREAT! THEN I WOULD SUGGEST THAT YOU CONTACT YOUR"
80 PRINT "LOCAL EXTENSION AGENT"
90 PRINT "FOR A COPY OF THE AGRONOMY HANDBOOK."
```

2 Title-Work

```
10 PRINT "WORK"
20 PRINT "WHAT IS YOUR OCCUPATION?"
30 INPUT A$
40 PRINT "I WAS EMPLOYED AS A "A$
50 PRINT "DO YOU LIKE YOUR JOB?"
60 INPUT B$
70 PRINT "I FELT THAT WAY, TOO."
80 END
```

Note: Remember to SAVE these programs before you LOAD them.

SUMMARY

The storage and retrieval of information are essential for the microcomputer to be a productive tool. The SAVE and LOAD commands allow the microcomputer user to store and reuse agricultural information. Remember, the SAVE and LOAD commands may vary among different manufacturers' microcomputers.

12

Using GOTO

This chapter introduces BASIC commands that can be used to repeat and manipulate computer instructions. These commands are GOTO, STOP, and CONT. STOP and CONT are useful in the development of longer and more complicated programs.

Objectives

1. Define GOTO, STOP, CONT, and BREAK KEY.
2. Review practice examples of how to use the GOTO, STOP, and CONT commands.
3. Determine when to use the BREAK KEY.
4. Write an agricultural-related program using the GOTO, STOP, and CONT commands as specified in the self-test.

One of the most powerful advantages of the microcomputer is its ability to repeat a task. The microprocessor can with magnificent speed perform a given set of instructions over and over. Together with the IF. . .THEN command, which is presented in Chapter 13, the GOTO command will allow you to instruct the microprocessor to repeat a set of instructions. The STOP and CONT (short for continue) commands allow you to delay a continuous program until you are ready to proceed or to make changes in a loop before it is repeated. A loop is a sequence of computer program instructions that will continue to be repeated until a present condition is met.

Figure 12-1
When used in combination with the PRINT and INPUT commands, the GOTO command will direct the microprocessor to a line in a program for the next set of facts or information. It can eliminate the need to RUN the program for each item to be analyzed.

Definitions

• **GOTO:** The GOTO (there may be a space between the GO and the TO) command allows the program to send the computer to a line out of numerical order.

• **STOP:** The STOP command will halt the program being run and return the control to the user.

• **CONT:** The CONT command is to continue the execution of the program that has been stopped. The CONT command may be used if a program has been stopped by using the STOP key (some machines), using the BREAK key, or an END statement within the program. This command will work only if no modification has been initiated in the program.

• **BREAK KEY**: Stops the running of the program.

========================**QUESTIONS AND ANSWERS**========================

QUESTION   After completion of the GOTO command, what will be the next line executed in the program?

ANSWER   The first command executed after GOTO is the one on the line listed after the GOTO statement. For example, when using GOTO 20, the microprocessor will execute the command *on* line 20 and all following commands.

QUESTION   How many times will the GOTO function be repeated?

ANSWER   Continuously, until the BREAK key or key to terminate function is needed.

QUESTION   How can I set up the program if the GOTO statement is to be executed a predetermined number of times?

ANSWER   This can be done by the use of other commands. The FOR command explained in Chapter 17 is for this use.

QUESTION   Can more than one GOTO statement be used in a program?

ANSWER   Yes; however, this requires the use of the IF ... THEN and END commands, which are presented in Chapter 13. So for now limit one per program and read on.

QUESTION   When can the BREAK or equivalent key be used?

ANSWER   Anytime you want to interrupt a program.

QUESTION   Can I get a program to continue after using a BREAK key?

ANSWER   No, except to RUN the program again. The BREAK key is used to stop the execution of a program.

QUESTION   What if my microcomputer keyboard does not have a BREAK key?

ANSWER   All microcomputers are designed to allow the operator to interrupt a microprocessor that is running on and on in an endless sequence or repeated instruction. Check the operating instructions of your microcomputer's manufacturer to determine the key or key combinations that will interrupt an operating program.

QUESTION   When using a STOP command, where will the program return to begin again?

ANSWER   To the next line following the STOP instruction line. A CONT command is necessary to restart the program after a STOP command.

QUESTION   Can other commands be executed or can the program be edited while the STOP command has interrupted the program?

ANSWER   Yes; in fact, the primary use of the STOP and CONT command is to edit and check the operations of a long program as it is being written. Remember these two for later use.

QUESTION   How can I start a STOPped program?

ANSWER   By using the CONT command. CONT is short for the word continue. After you enter the CONT command, the program will begin at the line immediately following the line of the STOP command.

QUESTION   Are STOP commands used frequently in finished programs?

ANSWER   Most STOP commands are deleted from the program after the final editing is complete.

══════════ PRACTICE EXAMPLES ══════════

Try the following to practice GOTO, STOP, CONT, and the BREAK key.

Remember, if you get an error message like ?SN? error, check Appendix E, which explains the error; then retype and enter the instruction correctly.

Commands: `10 PRINT "HELLO AGGIE"`
(new   `20 GOTO 10`
commands)

          Now RUN **this short program.**

Result: `HELLO AGGIE`
              `HELLO AGGIE`
              `HELLO AGGIE`
              `HELLO AGGIE`
              `HELLO AGGIE`

          The screen will fill up and continue to add `HELLO AGGIE` **until you press the** `[BREAK]` **or equivalent key to stop the program. If you are having trouble, turn the microcomputer off. Try a second time using the** BREAK **feature of your computer.**

Example 12-1

Let's continue, but this time we will use the GOTO command more sensibly. Command: Type NEW to erase the HELLO AGGIE program.

Command: `10 PRINT "A LIST OF FRIENDS"`
           `20 PRINT "WHAT IS THE NAME OF A FRIEND?"`
           `30 INPUT P$`
           `40 PRINT P$" IS A FRIEND."`
           `50 STOP`
(New
Command)   `60 GOTO 20`

Command: RUN — **the program**

Result: `A LIST OF FRIENDS`
           `WHAT IS THE NAME OF A FRIEND?`

Example 12-2

Command: Type in BILL or the name of a friend

Result: BILL IS A FRIEND.
           BREAK IN 50

                          The computer has interrupted the program in the line
                          containing the STOP instruction. To continue, type in
                          the CONT command and enter it.

Command: CONT (and enter)

Result: WHAT IS THE NAME OF A FRIEND?

                          The microprocessor continues by reading line 60 and
                          following the instructions to GOTO line 20. Once
                          again, the microprocessor is waiting for you to type in
                          a friend's name.

Command: Type in MARY or another friend's name

Result: MARY IS A FRIEND.
           BREAK IN 50

                          Once again the microprocessor has STOPped the
                          program where you asked it to STOP.
                          You may use the CONT command to go through the instruction
                          again or use the [BREAK] key to get out of the program.

Command: [BREAK] key

Result: The program is no longer operating.

Command: LIST to print on the screen the Friend program

Result: 10 PRINT "A LIST OF FRIENDS"
           20 PRINT "WHAT IS THE NAME OF A FRIEND?"
           30 INPUT P$
           40 PRINT P$" IS A FRIEND."
           50 STOP
           60 GOTO 20

Command: Type 50 as a program line; enter it

Command: LIST

Result: 10 PRINT "A LIST OF FRIENDS"
           20 PRINT "WHAT IS THE NAME OF A FRIEND?"
           30 INPUT P$
           40 PRINT P$" IS A FRIEND."
           60 GOTO 20

Command: RUN

Example 12-2   *(Continued)*

Result: A LIST OF FRIENDS
WHAT IS THE NAME OF A FRIEND?

Command: Type and enter BILL or other name

Result: BILL IS A FRIEND.
WHAT IS THE NAME OF A FRIEND?

> The microprocessor has followed the GOTO
> command by repeating line 20 after
> the PRINT command of line 40. You
> may enter as many names as you wish. Each time
> the microprocessor will complete the
> PRINT command of line 40 and
> repeat line 20.

Command: Use the (BREAK) key or control to interrupt the program

Result: BREAK IN 30

> Now you are free to LIST the program
> and RUN to try again or type NEW and
> move on to the next exercise!

Example 12-2 *(Continued)*

════════════ AGRICULTURAL APPLICATION ════════════

Type and enter the following program.

Command:
```
5 PRINT "FED CATTLE VALUE"
8 PRINT "ENTER FED ANIMAL'S ID?"
10 INPUT A$
14 PRINT "ENTER WEIGHT IN LBS."
15 INPUT A
20 PRINT "ENTER PRICE IN CENTS PER LB."
28 INPUT B
30 PRINT "FED VALUE OF-"A$"-IS $"A*B/100
35 STOP
40 GOTO 8
```

Command: RUN

Result: FED CATTLE VALUE
ENTER FED ANIMAL'S ID?

> The program waits for you to enter a test list of figures
> or letters. Try BOSSY;14.

Example 12-3

Command: Type in BOSSY;14

Result: ENTER WEIGHT IN LBS.

                                  The program waits for you to enter a number.
                                  Try 1125.

Command: Type in 1125

Result: ENTER PRICE IN CENTS PER LB.

                                  The program waits for you to enter a number;
                                  try 55.

Command: Type in 55

Result: FED VALUE OF BOSSY;14 IS $618.75
          BREAK IN 35

                                  The program has determined the value of the fed
                                  animal and has STOP**ped to see if you want to do**
                                  another animal calculation.

Command: **Type in** CONT

Result: ENTER FED ANIMAL'S ID?

                                  The program is repeating; enter an ID like
                                  STEER 47 **and** 975 **pounds and** 50
                                  cents. The calculation will be completed
                                  and a BREAK **in** 35 **will again appear.**
                                  This time type in 35 **with no instructions.**

Command: Type in 35 **as a line number and enter**

Command: Type RUN **and enter the command.**

                                  Now the program will continue to run
                                  through the cycle of instructions, which in
                                  programmer's language is referred to as a
                                  loop. **To get out of the loop, use the**
                                  BREAK **key.**

Command: BREAK **key**

Result: **The microprocessor is ready to receive another command;**
          try LIST **to check your program.**

Command: LIST
          5 PRINT 'FED CATTLE VALUE'
          8 PRINT 'ENTER FED ANIMAL'S ID?'

Example 12-3   *(Continued)*

```
10 INPUT A$
14 PRINT "ENTER WEIGHT IN LBS."
15 INPUT A
20 PRINT "ENTER PRICE IN CENTS PER LB.
28 INPUT B
30 PRINT "FED VALUE OF -"A$"-IS $"A*B/100
35 STOP
40 GOTO 8
```

Some microprocessors will leave line 35
listed but without any instruction. Most
machines will delete any line number that
does not have a command. In our case, the
STOP **and** CONT **commands were used**
to check to see if the program loop worked
before sending the microprocessor on the
continuous pattern back through the program.
If the program contains incorrect commands,
it can be altered when the STOP **command**
has interrupted the program.

If you want to RUN **the program again,**
remember to use the BREAK **feature to**
interrupt the program.

Example 12-3   *(Continued)*

═══════════════ **SELF-TEST EXAMPLES** ═══════════════

The following provide examples of GOTO using the STOP
and CONTinue feature to edit before running a loop.

1 Write a program that includes the STOP, CONT, edit
feature and includes a GOTO loop. Determine daily gain
for market hogs. Use entries for animal ID, days on feed,
and weight gained while on feed. Keep this program in
the microprocessor memory for use with example 2.

2 Remove the STOP and CONT edit features.

SUMMARY

The GOTO adds a new dimension to a program. GOTO can be used to repeat an entire set of instructions (called a loop) or branch to a subroutine. The STOP and CONT are useful to the program writer in trying out parts of a program and in developing longer, more complicated programs. The BREAK key interrupts or ends the execution of a program.

13

Try an IF . . . THEN Statement

The IF . . . THEN provides a degree of decision making that can be incorporated into a program. This flexibility is a benefit when there may be more than one answer to a given situation. With the use of an IF . . . THEN command, program alternatives will be selected only when criteria of the IF . . . THEN statement are satisfied.

Objectives

1. Define IF . . . THEN and REM.
2. Review the conditions under which the IF . . . THEN command is appropriate.
3. Try out the IF . . . THEN practice examples.
4. Write a program to include the IF . . . THEN command and REM as specified in the self-test.

By now you have mastered some of the direct commands of basic programming. The IF . . . THEN statement is a conditional command. The IF . . . THEN provides the microprocessor the capacity to proceed to one of two alternative computations. The IF . . . THEN statement will evaluate a condition and select the appropriate action from predetermined alternatives. The computer will make the appropriate choice.

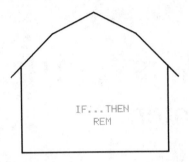

Figure 13-1
The IF command is followed by a statement of a condition. The microprocessor proceeds to the THEN command only when the condition statement is true or has been satisfied.

Definitions

. IF . . . THEN: The IF . . . THEN command provides for the evaluation of a condition or conditions and takes different action based on the outcome. The options that follow the IF command may include the expression of:

Variables	Numbers
Strings	Comparison

On the same line, following the IF command and its expression, there is a THEN command followed by more commands or a line number; the computer will make the evaluation. If the statement is true or appropriate, the computer will execute the THEN statement. When the expression is false or inappropriate, all components after the command THEN on that line are ignored, and the computer continues to the next numbered line in the program.

• **REM:** The REM is not a command and will not be read by the computer. The REM line can be employed to make the program more useful when it is LISTED.

═════════════════QUESTIONS AND ANSWERS═════════════════

QUESTION   What are the computer's symbols and capability to make decisions in the IF . . . THEN command?

ANSWER   The computer when commanded can determine the following:

$$= \text{ Equals}$$
$$> \text{ Greater than}$$
$$>= \quad \text{or} \quad => \text{ Greater than or equal to}$$
$$<= \quad \text{or} \quad =< \text{ Less than or equal to}$$
$$< \text{ Less than}$$
$$<> \quad \text{or} \quad >< \text{ Not equal to}$$
$$\text{AND Logical AND}$$
$$\text{OR Logical OR}$$
$$\text{NOT Logical NOT}$$

QUESTION   Can the IF . . . THEN command be used to evaluate an INPUT?

ANSWER   Yes; the computer will review the input statement and make the programmed decision.

QUESTION   What will the computer execute if, upon evaluation, the IF statement is incorrect or inappropriate?

ANSWER   The computer will go to the next numbered line of the program.

QUESTION   Can the IF . . . THEN command be used in the evaluation of strings and variables?

ANSWER   Either or both. The information must be exactly as it appears in the program. If strings and variables are INPUTted but not in the same *order* as they appear in the program, the THEN statement will be executed.

QUESTION   Can an IF . . . THEN command be used with a string variable?

ANSWER   Yes, but the characters input to be compared to the string variable must be placed in quotation marks.

QUESTION   What does the REM statement do?

ANSWER   The REM statement simply tells the computer to remember information for you.

QUESTION   When do I use a REM statement?

ANSWER   Anytime you have information you want to remember that is pertinent to your program. Most programs have REM statements that include the program name, author's name, date the program was written, and a definition of all variables used in the program.

QUESTION   What effects do REM statements have on my program while it is being run?

ANSWER   The computer completely ignores REM statements while it is running the program.

===================== PRACTICE EXAMPLE =====================

Try the following example to practice the use of the IF . . . THEN command. Remember to clear the computer's memory before starting this program. This will be achieved by turning the computer off or typing the command NEW to clear the memory. If while developing the program you produce a ?SX? or SYNTAX error, check to be sure that the line has been typed exactly as it is printed. If not, correct and enter again.

```
Command:  10 PRINT "PICK A NUMBER BETWEEN ONE AND FIVE."
          20 INPUT A
          30 IF A<>3 THEN PRINT "WRONG, TRY AGAIN":GOTO 10
          40 PRINT "GOOD, THE END."

Result:   PICK A NUMBER BETWEEN ONE AND FIVE.
```

> The computer has printed the instruction and has placed a "?" near the cursor for your input. It is only after the input that the computer can take the next step.

```
Enter:    2 (type and enter the number 2)
```

> The computer will compare 2 (your input) with the IF . . .; in this case it was <>, then 3, and the input was less, so the computer executes the THEN command.

```
Result:   PICK A NUMBER BETWEEN ONE AND FIVE.
          2
          WRONG, TRY AGAIN
          PICK A NUMBER BETWEEN ONE AND FIVE.

Enter:    3 (type and enter the number 3)

Result:   GOOD, THE END.
```

> The input was determined to be the correct number and so the computer ignored the THEN statement and went to the next line.

Example 13-1

The IF . . . THEN command can be used to assure that there will be reasonable input. Let us add our control to the Butterfat Calculation program.

=================== **AGRICULTURAL APPLICATION** ===================

Enter and run the following program.

```
Command:   10 PRINT "BUTTERFAT CALCULATION PROGRAM"
           20 PRINT "WHAT IS THE COW'S IDENTIFICATION NUMBER OR NAME?"
           25 INPUT C$
           29 PRINT "WHAT IS THE COW'S PRODUCTION?"
           35 INPUT A
           40 PRINT "WHT IS THE COW'S BUTTERFAT TEST?"
           43 INPUT B
           45 IF B>15 THEN 60
           50 PRINT "COW-"C$"-BUTTERFAT PRODUCTION IS,"A*B/100"-POUNDS
              OF FAT":GOTO 70
           60 PRINT "COWS DO NOT NORMALLY PRODUCE MORE THAN 15%
              BUTTERFAT. CHECK DATA AND RERUN PROGRAM."
           70 PRINT"THE END":END

Result:    RUN
```

> The program will run exactly as it did before until
> it reaches line 45. If the INPUT is greater than
> 15 (IF B>15), the THEN statement will
> be executed and the computer screen will read:

```
COWS DO NOT NORMALLY PRODUCE MORE THAN 15% BUTTERFAT.
CHECK DATA AND RERUN PROGRAM.
THE END
```

> Without this kind of control any information
> INPUTted will be computed. The computer
> does not know that the butterfat range for dairy
> animals is 3% to 6%. It will compute any input.

Example 13-2

══════════════ SELF-TEST EXAMPLE ══════════════

1 Revise self-test example 2 from Chapter 10, which allows an
input of 60 or more days on feed. The problem would read:

Set up a series of one text input and two number input
statements that calculates the daily weight gain of steer
Joe-74 whose weight was 300 pounds when purchased and
975 pounds at market. There were 60 or more days between
beginning weight and market time.

SUMMARY

Remember, the REM is simply a note to the programmer or person reviewing a set of instructions. REM is ignored in the RUN of a program. The IF . . . THEN is a powerful command that provides alternative directions within a program.

14

GOSUB/RETURN

The GOSUB command allows more flexibility than the GOTO command by providing a way for the microcomputer to execute a subroutine and then continue the program. The RETURN command provides the means for the microcomputer to go back to the point following the GOSUB and continue the RUN of the program.

Objectives

1. Learn the function of GOSUB/RETURN.
2. Review the GOSUB/RETURN practice example.
3. Apply the GOSUB/RETURN to an agricultural program.
4. Write a program to include the GOSUB/RETURN command as specified in the self-test.

The GOSUB command allows you to move from one line in the program into any subroutine. This is very similar to the GOTO command except you have flexibility when using the GOSUB command with the RETURN command. The GOSUB/RETURN commands remember the line at which the GOSUB was initiated and the RETURN command simply returns the pointer back to the line number immediately following the origin of the GOSUB command.

Figure 14-1
GOSUB allows subroutine programs within a program to be executed and then RETURN to continue the program at the line immediately following the GOSUB command.

Definitions

• **GOSUB:** The GOSUB command is a specialized form of the GOTO command. The GOSUB command remembers where it came from, and when it has completed its task and when a RETURN command is included, the computer will automatically return to the next line in the program immediately following the GOSUB statement from which it came.

• **RETURN:** The RETURN command is used in conjunction with the GOSUB command. Upon reading the RETURN command, the program returns to the next numbered line after the GOSUB command.

• **END:** The END command stops the program and tells the computer there are no further statements in the program. The END command must, therefore, be the last statement in the BASIC program. The END statement includes a line number and the word END.

QUESTIONS AND ANSWERS

QUESTION   How does the GOSUB command differ from the GOTO command?

ANSWER   The GOSUB command allows the programmer to execute a subroutine and return to the line number immediately following the GOSUB command.

QUESTION   When should a GOSUB command be used?

ANSWER   If a particular line or instruction is used over and over again in a program, the GOSUB command should be utilized.

QUESTION   Is the RETURN command the same as the RETURN key?

ANSWER   No, the RETURN key enters the command into the CPU memory. The RETURN command is used in conjunction with the GOSUB command.

QUESTION   What would happen if you used a GOSUB without a RETURN command?

ANSWER   You would get an error message: RETURN WITHOUT GOSUB ERROR.

QUESTION   What does the RETURN command do?

ANSWER   When executing a program and the program hits a RETURN command, the pointer will go to the line number immediately following the GOSUB command.

QUESTION   What does the END command do?

ANSWER   This command tells the computer that the program has been completed.

QUESTION   Is the END command always placed at the end of a listed program?

ANSWER   No; the END command should be placed before
the loops in the program. This will prevent the
computer from executing the GOSUB loops
placed at the end of the program.

PRACTICE EXAMPLE

Type and run the following program.

```
10 PRINT "CALCULATING BOARD FEET"
20 PRINT "HOW MANY FEET ARE IN A BOARD 2 INCHES BY 12 INCHES
   BY 20 FEET?"
25 GOSUB 200
30 INPUT A$
40 IF A$<>"40" THEN PRINT "SORRY, TRY AGAIN":GOTO 20
50 PRINT "GREAT, YOU GOT IT"
60 PRINT "YOU NEED TO RECONSTRUCT A 15 BY 20 FOOT FLOOR."
70 PRINT "YOU MUST USE 2 INCHES BY 10 INCHES BY 10 FEET LUMBER."
80 PRINT "HOW MANY BOARD FEET WILL BE NEEDED TO CONSTRUCT THE FLOOR?"
90 GOSUB 200
100 INPUT B$
110 IF B$<>"600" THEN PRINT "SORRY, WRONG ANSWER - TRY AGAIN":GOTO 60
120 PRINT "GREAT, YOU GOT IT!"
130 PRINT "THE END"
140 END
200 PRINT "THE FORMULA FOR CALCULATING BOARD FEET IS
    LENGTH x WIDTH x THICKNESS."
210 PRINT "NOTE: A BOARD 1 INCH BY 12 INCHES BY 12 INCHES = 1 BD. FT."
220 RETURN
```

Example 14-1

AGRICULTURAL EXAMPLES

Type and run the following program.

```
10 PRINT "FIELD SIZE"
20 PRINT "HOW LONG IS THE FIELD?"
25 PRINT "(TYPE NUMBER & PRESS ENTER)"
30 INPUT A
50 PRINT "HOW WIDE IS THE FIELD?"
55 PRINT "(TYPE NUMBER & PRESS ENTER)"
60 INPUT B
80 C=(A*B)/43560
90 PRINT "THE FIELD CONTAINS "C" ACRES."
100 END
```

Example 14-2

Now let's try a GOSUB and a RETURN:

```
10 PRINT "FIELD SIZE"
20 PRINT "HOW LONG IS THE FIELD?"
25 GOSUB 150
30 INPUT A
50 PRINT "HOW WIDE IS THE FIELD?"
55 GOSUB 150
60 INPUT B
80 C=(A*B)/43560
90 PRINT "THE FIELD CONTAINS "C" ACRES."
100 END
150 PRINT "(TYPE NUMBER & PRESS ENTER)"
160 RETURN
```

Example 14-3

SELF-TEST EXAMPLE

1 Modify the following program to include a GOSUB command and a RETURN command.

```
10 PRINT "DETERMINE FIELD SIZE"
20 PRINT "CALCULATING THE NUMBER OF ACRES IN A RECTANGULAR FIELD."
30 PRINT "HOW LONG (IN FEET) IS THE FIELD?"
35 PRINT "TYPE IN THE NUMBER AND PRESS ENTER TO CONTINUE."
40 INPUT A
50 PRINT "HOW WIDE (IN FEET) IS THE FIELD?"
55 PRINT "TYPE IN THE NUMBER AND PRESS ENTER TO CONTINUE."
60 INPUT B
70 C=(A*B)/43560
80 PRINT "THE FIELD CONTAINS"C"ACRES."
90 END
```

SUMMARY

Programs within a program can be achieved through the use of the GOSUB and RETURN. The RETURN must be placed within the subroutine of the GOSUB.

LET and Clear Screen

The LET command explained in this chapter is used to simplify a complicated numerical or word function. Another command, Clear the Screen, in the execution of a program provides a pleasing and more functional display of a program.

Objective

1. Determine the purpose of the LET.
2. Identify the Clear Screen command.
3. Complete the LET and Clear Screen practice examples.
4. Write an agricultural-related program to include a LET and Clear Screen as outlined in the self-test.

The addition of a LET statement will shorten many programs. It is particularly useful when a part of a repeating routine is to remain at a constant value.

The command that clears the video screen at a prescribed point within a program is used to remove extraneous information from the screen. It is especially effective when a new item is being analyzed or when used between input statements that are collecting information to solve a problem.

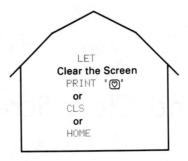

Figure 15-1
The Clear the Screen command is often different with each machine. Check the operator's handbook for your computer's clear command.

Definitions

• **LET:** The LET command can be used to set a variable to a value in the form of a number (like 7) or letter (like C) or a formula (like C=A+B). Some microcomputers do not require the word LET.

• **PRINT" ♡ ", CLS, HOME:** These clear screen commands are used to remove all written material from the screen not the memory.

═══════════ **QUESTIONS AND ANSWERS** ═══════════

QUESTION   What is the difference between the commands LET B$ = "HORSE" and B$ = "HORSE"?

ANSWER   It depends on the form that your microprocessor is designed to accept. Try each form and see which works for you. (Consult your user's manual.)

QUESTION   Is the LET command similar to an INPUT command?

ANSWER   Yes; both commands ask for information that is to be used later when called for.

QUESTION   Does it matter where the LET statement is positioned within a program?

ANSWER   Yes, it must be in a position where it can be read into the microprocessor prior to when it will be called from memory for use in solving a problem.

QUESTION   Why is a Clear the Screen function typically found as the first instruction of a program?

ANSWER   Mostly to make a more attractive and more easily understood program. The Clear the Screen function removes all video symbols that may be left by previous instructions.

QUESTION   Can I delay the Clear the Screen function for a specified time?

ANSWER   Yes; in a later chapter the FOR statement will be used to delay the microprocessor by having it count. Also, some microprocessors may have a time function that can be set to delay the completion of a program by parts of a second or for minutes or even hours.

================ PRACTICE EXAMPLES ================

This is the last in a series of introductory practice examples. Use of the LET and Clear commands will give your programming efforts a more professional appearance.

Type and run the following programs.

```
Command:  10 PRINT "BASKETBALL SCORE AVERAGES"
          20 PRINT "ENTER POINTS SCORED GAME 1"
          25 INPUT A
          30 PRINT "ENTER POINTS AGAINST GAME 1"
          35 INPUT B
```

Example 15-1

```
40 PRINT "ENTER POINTS SCORED GAME 2"
45 INPUT C
50 PRINT "ENTER POINTS AGAINST GAME 2"
55 INPUT D
60 LET F=(A+C)/2
65 LET G=(B+D)/2
70 IF F<G THEN 100
75 PRINT "THE AVERAGE WINNING MARGIN WAS "F-G" POINTS"
80 END
100 PRINT "THE AVERAGE LOSING MARGIN WAS "G-F" POINTS"
```

As you can see, the LET statement can create
new items by combining INPUT information.
Item F when called for later in the program will
be the average points scored in games 1 and 2.

Some microprocessors do not require the word
LET to proceed the new item. If your machine
indicates an error in line 60, try omitting the
word LET; type in F=(A+C)/2. Change line 65
in the same way. (Check your user's manual.)

Command: RUN

Result: BASKETBALL SCORE AVERAGES
                 ENTER POINTS SCORED GAME 1

Command: **Type in** 85 **and continue**
                 ENTER POINTS AGAINST GAME 1
                 Type in 64 **and continue**
                 ENTER POINTS SCORED GAME 2
                 Type in 75 **and continue**
                 ENTER POINTS AGAINST GAME 2
                 Type in 74 **and continue**

Result: THE AVERAGE WINNING MARGIN WAS 11 POINTS

Try several combinations to see
what happens.

Keep this program in memory for the next practice exercise.

Example 15-1   *(Continued)*

Additional LET statements can be added to
create items that represent the average winning
or losing score. Try the following.

Example 15-2

Command: LIST the program
          Add the following instruction lines
          67 LET H=F-G
          69 LET I=G-F

                        Now you can simplify lines 75 **and** 100 **by**
                        making the following changes:

          75 PRINT "THE AVERAGE WINNING MARGIN WAS,"H",POINTS"
          100 PRINT "THE AVERAGE LOSING MARGIN WAS,"I",POINTS"

Command: RUN

Result: **Add input items as called for. The result will be the same as in**
          the previous exercise. Just a little more practice using LET
          statements.

Again, save this program for the next exercise.

Example 15-2   *(Continued)*

The following example shows a typical clean-up job.

Most professionally designed programs will clear
the screen of all information as a program starts.
Next a title will appear and disappear followed by
questions asking for information. After all the
information is gathered, again the screen will be
cleared. The results will be reported again on a
clear screen. This exercise will demonstrate how
to clean up your screen.

Command: 5 CLS **or** PRINT " ♡ " **or** HOME

The clear the screen command will vary according
to the microprocessor manufacturer. Try the
above; if it does not work, check with the
instruction manual or your dealer.

          12 STOP

The line 5 command will clear the screen to
start the program. Line 12 will keep the title,
line 10 BASKETBALL SCORE AVERAGES, **on**
the screen until the CONT command is entered.

Example 15-3

```
18 CLS or PRINT "⟨♡⟩" or HOME
```

Again the screen is cleared. The INPUT
statements will follow.

```
58 CLS or PRINT "⟨♡⟩" or HOME
```

Once more the screen is cleared. This time the
results will appear on the screen as the only item.

Command: LIST the program to check for errors

Command: RUN and add inputs

Result: The screen should be cleared three times. First, at the beginning
           of the program, second, after the title is shown and the CONT
           command is entered, third, after input data are entered. The
           result is a more easily understood program.

Example 15-3   *(Continued)*

AGRICULTURAL APPLICATION

This example will give you an idea of how to write programs that
can determine costs and returns of an agricultural commodity.

```
Command:   5 CLS
           10 PRINT "ECONOMICS OF CITRUS GROVES"
           12 PRINT "TO BEGIN ENTER YES"
           14 INPUT C$
           16 IF C$="YES" THEN 18
           18 CLS
           20 PRINT "ENTER INSECTICIDE COST PER ACRE"
           25 INPUT A
           30 PRINT "ENTER FERTILIZER COST PER ACRE"
           35 INPUT B
           40 PRINT "ENTER COST OF WATER (5 IRRIGATIONS) PER ACRE"
           45 INPUT C
           50 PRINT "ENTER PRUNING LABOR COST PER ACRE"
           55 INPUT D
           60 PRINT "ENTER IRRIGATION LABOR COST PER ACRE"
           65 INPUT F
           70 PRINT "ENTER ANNUAL TRACTOR COST"
           75 INPUT G
           80 PRINT "ENTER ANNUAL SPRAYER COST"
           85 INPUT H
           90 PRINT "WHAT IS THE EXPECTED YIELD IN TONS OF
              FRESH ORANGES PER ACRE?"
```

Example 15-4

```
95 INPUT I
100 PRINT "WHAT IS EXPECTED FRESH PRICE PER TON?"
105 INPUT J
110 PRINT "WHAT IS THE EXPECTED YIELD IN TONS OF PROCESSED
    ORANGES PER ACRE?"
115 INPUT K
116 PRINT "WHAT IS PROCESSED ORANGE PRICE PER TON?"
118 INPUT N
120 CLS
125 LET M=A+B+C
128 LET L=D+F
130 LET E=G+H
135 LET Y=I*J
140 LET W=K*N
145 LET V=Y+W
148 LET Z=M+L+E
150 PRINT "MATERIAL COST PER ACRE IS $"M
155 PRINT "LABOR COST PER ACRE IS $"L
160 PRINT "EQUIPMENT COST PER ACRE IS $"E
165 PRINT "TOTAL COST PER ACRE IS $"Z
170 PRINT "FRESH RETURN PER ACRE IS $"Y
175 PRINT "PROCESSED RETURN PER ACRE IS $"W
180 PRINT "TOTAL RETURN PER ACRE IS $"V
185 IF V<Z THEN 210
190 PRINT "PROFIT PER ACRE IS $"V-Z
200 PRINT "TO DO ANOTHER CALCULATION ENTER 1;
    IF NOT ENTER 2":INPUT R
205 IF R = 1 THEN 5
208 END
210 PRINT "LOSS PER ACRE IS $Z-V

220 PRINT "TO DO ANOTHER CALCULATION ENTER 1;
    IF NOT ENTER 2":INPUT R
225 IF R = 1 THEN 5
230 END
```

LIST **the program to check lines for accuracy.
Then run with the following information:**

Insecticide	200
Fertilizer	90
Water	22
Pruning	12
Water labor	56
Tractor	25
Sprayer	54
Fresh orange	12
Fresh price	175
Processed orange	9
Processed price	110

Example 15-4 *(Continued)*

Result: The program will print the following on the screen:

```
MATERIAL COST PER ACRE IS $312
LABOR COST PER ACRE IS $68
EQUIPMENT COST PER ACRE IS $79
TOTAL COST PER ACRE IS $459
FRESH RETURN PER ACRE IS $2100
PROCESSED RETURN PER ACRE IS $990
TOTAL RETURN PER ACRE IS $3090
PROFIT PER ACRE IS $2631
TO DO ANOTHER CALCULATION ENTER 1; IF NOT ENTER 2
```

Command: `ENTER 2`

Let's try a year with a hurricane that reduced yields 1 ton of fresh oranges and 2 tons of processed oranges.

Result: `LOSS PER ACRE IS $64`

The advantage of a program of this type to an agriculturalist is the ability to keep the program on a storage device and then use it at anytime it appears that one of the input items will change. The result is an immediate estimate of the impact that the change may have on profit or loss.

Also, you may want to add a clear the screen command between some of the print statements.

Otherwise, type `NEW` or store this program for a later look. Proceed to the self-test example and design your own cost analysis program.

Example 15-4 *(Continued)*

SELF-TEST EXAMPLES

1 Write a program that will call for the following income and expense items and determine total profit or loss in the farm feed and supply store business.

   a. Monthly Labor Expenses
      Salesperson, $1000 plus 2% of sales
      Janitorial (part-time), $200
      General helper, $900

   b. Materials Sold Expenses
      Feed, $120 per ton (average 100 tons per month)
      Appliances, $4000 average per month expense
   c. Fixed and Building Costs
      Electricity, $125 per month
      Heating and cooling, $150 per month
   d. Monthly Income
      Feed, $180 per ton (average 99 tons sold)
      Appliances, $5000 average per month receipts

   Include a monthly reporting statement of the following:

      Labor expenses
      Materials sold expenses
      Fixed and building expenses
      Feed income
      Appliances income
      Total expenses
      Total income
      Profit or loss

2 Alter the farm feed and supply store program to report the
  annual statement. Include an annual report statement for
  the following:

      Labor expenses
      Materials sold expenses
      Fixed and building expenses
      Feed income
      Appliances income
      Total income
      Total expenses
      Annual profit or loss

  This time include Clear the Screen and a delay between the
  new annual expense reporting print statements and the
  monthly statements. *Hint:* There are two commands you
  have learned to do this with:

                    -STOP & CONT or
             INPUT and IF statement

Later you will learn how to use the FOR/NEXT commands to create a time delay. Also some machines may have a TIMER function within the microprocessor's memory.

SUMMARY

The LET is used to assign a value to a variable title. LET is not recognized by all microcomputers. The Clear Screen is useful in the development of an easy to read display of information. Remember, Clear the Screen commands vary by microcomputer manufacturer.

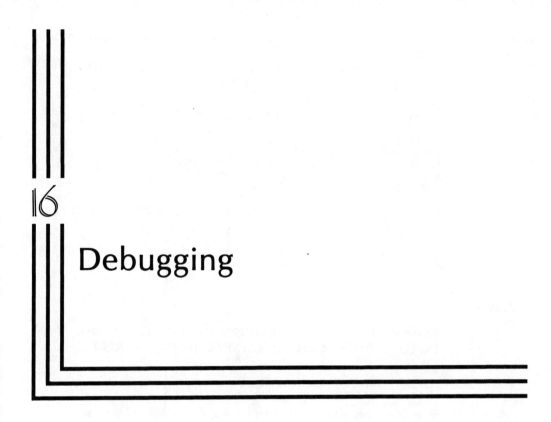

16

Debugging

The programs presented in this chapter will allow you the opportunity to reaffirm your ability to identify and correct errors within programs. Correct the errors in the following programs. In the first and second program, the errors will be listed. The third program will be filled with errors.

Objective

1. Correct the errors in three example programs.

Locate and correct the errors in the following programs.

Program I

This program contains errors in lines 10, 30, 80, 95, 120, and 170.

```
10 PRINT CALCULATING THE NUMBER OF ACRES IN A FIELD."
20 PRINT "HOW LONG (FEET) IS THE FIELD?"
25 GOSUB 150
30 INPUT A$
50 PRINT "HOW WIDE (FEET) IS THE FIELD?"
55 GOSUB 150
60 INPUT B
80 C=(A*B$)/43560
90 PRINT "THE FIELD CONTAINS " C "ACRES"
95 IF "C" >100 THEN PRINT C " ACRES IS A LARGE FIELD."
100 END
120 GOSUB 150
150 PRINT "TYPE IN THE NUMBER AND PRESS ENTER TO CONTINUE"
160 RETURN
170 END
```

Program II

Review the program and correct the following errors: PRINT, INPUT, IF-THEN, GOTO, GOSUB/RETURN, and REM.

```
5 PRINT "CORN PLANTING SOIL TEMPERATURES"
10 PRINT "WHAT TEMPERATURE" IS NEEDED FOR CORN SEED GERMINATIONPRINT"
20 INPUT A$
30 IF "A" <>55 THEN PRINT "WRONG ANSWER, TRY AGAIN":GOTO 60
40 PRINT "YOU ARE CORRECT."
50 PRINT "SOIL TEMPERATURES BELOW 55 CAN CAUSE POOR GERMINATION."
60 GOSUB 2100
70 REM FRED WAS HERE
150 END
2000 FOR X = 1 TO 1000:NEXT
2010 PRINT "GOOD ANSWER!"
2100 RETURN
```

Program III

Correct the following program.

```
10 PRINT "SPRAYING"
20 PRINT "THIS PROGRAM CAN HELP YOU CALCULATE TOTAL SPRAY VOLUME PER ACRE"
30 PRINT "FOR A BROADCAST SPRAYER."
40 PRINT "PRESS (RETURN) TO CONTINUE..."
50 INPUT A
60 PRINT SPRAY A TEST STRIP 660 FEET LONG AND MEASURE WATER USAGE."
80 PRINT "YOU WILL NEED TO KNOW THE"
90 PRINT "WIDTH (FEET) OF YOUR SPRAYER."
100 PRINT "DO YOU HAVE THE NEEDED INFORMATION?"
110 PRINT "ENTER Y FOR YES OR N FOR NO (AND PRESS RETURN)"
120 INPUT B$
130 IF B = "N" THEN 300
```

```
140 PRINT "HOW WIDE A SWATH DOES YOUR SPRAYER MAKE (FEET)?"
150 GOSUB 350
160 INPUT A$
170 PRINT "HOW MUCH WATER DID YOU USE IN THE TEST STRIP (GALLONS)?"
180 GOSUB 350
190 INPUT B
200 LET C = 66*(B/A)
210 PRINT "AT THE PRESENT CALIBRATION -- YOUR SPRAYER"
220 PRINT "DELIVERS "C" GALLONS OF SPRAY MATERIAL (VOLUME) PER ACRE."
230 GOTO 350
300 PRINT "THEN YOU SHOULD LEAVE NOW TO GET THAT INFORMATION."
310 PRINT "THE PROGRAM HAS ENDED FOR NOW."
320 PRINT "YOU CAN START AT THE BEGINNING WHEN YOU RETURN."
330 PRINT "  --THE END--  "
340 END
350 PRINT "ENTER NUMBER AND PRESS (RETURN)"
360 RETURN
```

SUMMARY

Correction of the errors in three example programs provided an opportunity to reaffirm your knowledge of the commands learned thus far in this text. Debugging a program will give you greater confidence.

17

FOR/NEXT

The FOR and NEXT commands are used to complement each other. The NEXT cannot function without the FOR. To create a loop using the FOR, there must be a NEXT at the end of the loop. A combination of the LET, IF, and GOTO commands can perform the same function as FOR/NEXT. The FOR/NEXT combination is more efficient.

Objectives

1. Learn the FOR and NEXT commands.
2. Illustrate the practice examples of FOR and NEXT.
3. Modify the self-test program to include a repeat loop using the FOR/NEXT.

The computer has the capacity to repeat a task by using the FOR command. The same process can usually be achieved without the FOR command, but it is more difficult to program and requires more lines.

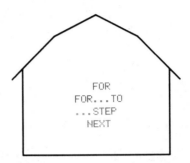

Figure 17-1
The FOR command is provided to allow the programmer to repeat the use of variable. The programmer must establish the variable name, identify the starting value, limit the repetitions and establish the quantity to be added during each cycle.

Definitions

• **FOR:** The FOR command is provided to allow the programmer to repeat a variable. The programmer must establish the variable name, identify the starting value, limit the repetitions, and establish the quantity to be added during each cycle.

• **FOR . . . TO:** Creates a loop in the program that must be repeated from the first to the last number.

• **NEXT:** The NEXT command is used to complete the loop that was initiated by the FOR command.

=================== **QUESTIONS AND ANSWERS** ===================

QUESTION   What variable can be used?

ANSWER   Any numeric variable name except an array variable can be used.

QUESTION   What does the computer do if there is no step command?

ANSWER The computer assumes there is a +1 step if none is listed.

QUESTION Can steps of various ranges be included in the FOR command?

ANSWER Yes, the computer can be instructed to take either positive (+1) or negative (−1) steps or fractions thereof (e.g., step +.02).

QUESTION How can the microcomputer be used as a timer?

ANSWER The microcomputer will count a certain number of beats per second.

QUESTION How many beats does the microcomputer count per second?

ANSWER The number of beats per second varies by microcomputer. Check the owner's handbook for the exact number of beats.

===================== **PRACTICE EXAMPLES** =====================

Execute the following examples to establish a clear understanding of the FOR command and its use.

The microcomputer can be commanded to list a sequence of numbers.

Command:
```
20 FOR N = 1 to 5
30 PRINT N
40 NEXT N
50 END
```

Result: **type** RUN
```
1
2
3
4
5
```

Example 17-1

There is a line number (20) and the FOR command. The = 1 to 5 instructs the microcomputer to start with the advance to 5; as there is no step statement the microcomputer assumes an increment of +1 and subsequently prints a list of numbers from 1 to 5. The microcomputer process functions internally like this after the STEP has been added to the variable, in this illustration 1+1; it is compared to the limit. In this illustration the limit is 5. If the limit has not been exceeded (1 + 1 = 2, which does not exceed 5), the program continues with the line after the FOR command. If the microcomputer determines that the limit has been exceeded (e.g., if it ever were 5 + 1), the microcomputer will move to the line that follows the NEXT command. In our illustration it is line 50. Without the NEXT command the microcomputer would not understand what to do when it reaches a count of 5 in our illustration.

Command: 20 FOR P = 1 to 20 STEP 4
                30 PRINT P
                40 NEXT P
                50 END

Result: **Type** RUN
                1
                5
                9
                13
                17

The microcomputer then listed the numbers within the range of 1 to 2 of 4 (i.e., 1 + 4 = *5* + 4 = *13* + 4 = *17* + 4 is more than 20 and so is omitted). The computer will accommodate a negative number by rewriting line 20 as follows:

Command: 20 FOR P = 20 TO 1 STEP −4
                30 PRINT P
                40 NEXT P
                50 END

Try it; see how it operates.

Example 17-1 *(Continued)*

Try this program on the TRS-80 computer.

```
Command:   10 FOR T=1 to 460*2
           20 NEXT T
           30 PRINT "THAT TOOK APPROXIMATELY TWO SECONDS"

Result:    Type RUN
           THAT TOOK APPROXIMATELY TWO SECONDS
```

> The microcomputer counts at a rate of so many beats per second. Line 10 instructed the computer to count from 1 to 460 two times (*2). Then it reported. The time component can be increased by increasing the count. The microcomputer can be instructed to count hours, minutes, or seconds.

Example 17-2

The FOR command will be critical to the DATA statement and will be used extensively in later chapters.

AGRICULTURAL APPLICATION

The FOR command as a time delay can be used to allow time to consider the possible answer. Consider the following example.
Type and run the following program:

```
10 PRINT "BUTTERFAT CALCULATION PROGRAM."
15 GOSUB 75
20 PRINT "WHAT IS THE COW'S IDENTIFICATION NUMBER OR NAME?"
25 INPUT C$
28 GOSUB 75
29 PRINT "WHAT IS THE COW'S PRODUCTION?"
35 INPUT A
38 GOSUB 75
40 PRINT "WHAT IS THE COW'S BUTTERFAT TEST?"
43 INPUT B
45 GOSUB 75
50 PRINT "COW-"C$"-BUTTERFAT PRODUCTION IS, "A*B/100" POUNDS OF FAT"
60 PRINT "THE END"
70 END
```

Example 17-3

```
75 PRINT
90 RETURN
```

Command: **Now type line:** 80 FORT=1 to 460: NEXT T

Result: The program will run exactly like it did before except there will be
                an approximate 1-second delay at line 80 in the program. All other
                activities will be the same.

Example 17-3 *(Continued)*

```
10 PRINT"BUTTERFAT CALCULATION PROGRAM."
15 GOSUB 75
20 PRINT"WHAT IS THE COW'S IDENTIFICATION NUMBER OR NAME?"
25 INPUT C$
28 GOSUB 75
29 PRINT "WHAT IS THE COW'S PRODUCTION?"
35 INPUT A
38 GOSUB 75
40 PRINT"WHAT IS THE COW'S BUTTERFAT TEST?"
43 INPUT B
45 GOSUB 75
50 PRINT"COW-"C$"-BUTTERFAT PRODUCTION IS, "A*B/100"POUNDS OF FAT"
60 PRINT "THE END"
70 END
75 PRINT
80 FOR T = 1 TO 460:NEXT T
90 RETURN
```

Example 17-4

========================= SELF-TEST EXAMPLE =========================

1 Add line 12 to the program on steer weight in the Chapter 13
self-test. Include a '1 to 1500' time delay for line 12:

$$12 \text{ FOR } X = 1 \text{ to } 1500: \text{ NEXT}$$

```
10 PRINT "STEER WEIGHT GAIN CALCULATION"
15 PRINT "ENTER THE STEER ID"
20 INPUT A$
30 PRINT "ENTER BEGINNING WEIGHT"
40 INPUT F
```

```
45 PRINT "ENTER MARKET WEIGHT"
50 INPUT H
55 PRINT "ENTER DAYS ON FEED - MUST EXCEED 60"
60 INPUT J
65 IF J < 60 THEN PRINT "MUST EXCEED 60 DAYS":GOTO 55
70 PRINT "DAILY GAIN OF STEER, "A$" WAS "(H-F)/J" POUNDS."
```

SUMMARY

The FOR and NEXT create a loop for the purpose of calculating or reading a set of variables. Remember, other commands such as GOTO, IF, and LET used together can do the same function as the FOR/NEXT, but the FOR/NEXT command is more efficient.

18

DATA/READ

This chapter discusses how data can be stored in one location within a program. The DATA and READ commands are used to locate and read information. The application of DATA and READ commands is useful when working with many variables.

Objectives

1. Learn the function of the DATA and READ.
2. Complete the practice examples of DATA and READ.
3. Complete the self-test to determine the results of the DATA and READ commands.

The DATA command is used when variables are stored within a program. The READ command works with the DATA command to read the variables located in DATA.

Figure 18-1
DATA stores information used in a program. READ
reads the DATA.

Definitions

• **DATA:** The DATA command is used to hold information
that will be used to fill variables in a READ command. Any type of
information may be stored if separated by commas.

• **READ:** The READ command instructs the computer to
READ the DATA values stored in the program to fill variables.
READ assigns data to variables.

═══════════ **QUESTIONS AND ANSWERS** ═══════════

QUESTION   What can be classified as DATA?

ANSWER   Data may be a word(s), number(s), graphics, or
             anything representing variables.

QUESTION   Must there be a READ command with a DATA
             command?

ANSWER   Yes, the READ command is similar to the INPUT
             command. The READ allows the variables placed
             in DATA to be utilized and read into the
             program.

QUESTION   How do I put data in a data statement?

ANSWER Simply give a line number, label the statement DATA, and list the data with commas between each item of data.

QUESTION How do data statements with character data (words or graphics) differ from data statements with numbers?

ANSWER Character data may be placed in quotation marks on most machines.

QUESTION Where are DATA statements placed in the program?

ANSWER DATA statements may be placed anywhere in the program. However, they are normally placed at the end of the program.

QUESTION What will happen if you have DATA without a READ command?

ANSWER The DATA must have a READ command in order for the DATA to be used in the program.

QUESTION How does the READ command differ from the INPUT command?

ANSWER READ works just like INPUT, except the information comes from DATA instead of the person running the program.

========================= **PRACTICE EXAMPLES** =========================

Type and run the following program.

```
Command:  10 PRINT 'AGES'
          20 DATA 85,90,94,91,100
          30 DATA 90,70,60,80,90
          40 DATA 80,60,90,90,80
          50 FOR X = 1 TO 15
          60 READ A
```

Example 18-1

```
                70 PRINT A
                80 NEXT

Results:        AGES
                85
                90
                94
                91
                100
                90
                70
                60
                80
                90
                80
                60
                90
                90
                80
```

Example 18-1 *(Continued)*

Type and run the following program.

```
Command:  10 PRINT "AGES"
          20 DATA 85,90,94,91,100
          30 DATA 90,70,60,80,90
          40 DATA 80,60,90,90,80
          50 FOR X = 1 TO 3
          60 READ A,B,C,D,E
          70 PRINTA,B,C,D,E
          80 NEXT

Results:  AGES
          85          90          94          91          100
          90          70          60          80          90
          80          60          90          90          80
```

Example 18-2

═══════════════ **AGRICULTURAL APPLICATION** ═══════════════

Try this program.

```
Command:  10 PRINT 'N-P-K'
          20 FOR X = TO 3
          30 READ A$,B$
          40 PRINT 'THE NUTRIENT DEFICIENCY SYMPTOM FOR 'A$' IS ' B$
          50 NEXT
          60 DATA NITROGEN,YELLOW LOWER LEAVES
          70 DATA PHOSPHORUS,RED PURPLE LEAVES
          80 DATA POTASSIUM,DEAD SPOTS ON LEAVES

Results:  THE NUTRIENT DEFICIENCY SYMPTOM FOR NITROGEN IS
             YELLOW LOWER LEAVES
          THE NUTRIENT DEFICIENCY SYMPTOM FOR PHOSPHORUS IS
             RED PURPLE LEAVES
          THE NUTRIENT DEFICIENCY SYMPTOM FOR POTASSIUM IS
             DEAD SPOTS ON LEAVES
```

Example 18-3

================= SELF-TEST EXAMPLES =================

1 What will the following program print?

```
10 FOR X = 1 TO 4
20 READ A
30 PRINT A
40 NEXT X
50 DATA 75,85
60 DATA 95,99
```

2 What will the following program print?

```
5 PRINT "SCORE 1","SCORE 2"
10 DATA 75,85
20 DATA 95,99
30 FOR X = 1 TO 2
40 READ A,B
50 PRINT A,B
60 NEXT
```

3 Write a program using DATA and READ to set up a table to include test scores for Fred, Joe, Jay, Tom, Jim, and Bob.

The test scores are 99, 88, 95, 96, 98, and 85. Use the following READ command: READ A$, A, B$, A, C$, C.

SUMMARY

DATA can be stored in one location and read when needed as input information through the use of the READ command. Remember, even though the DATA has been READ, it will not be displayed without a PRINT command. Also, information being stored in one location eliminates the need for many INPUT commands.

19

RESTORE

RESTORE will be discussed as a command that adds a greater influence to the DATA command. The ability of information stored in DATA to be used many times over is a product of RESTORE.

Objectives

1. Learn the function of RESTORE.
2. Define OD ERROR.
3. Define CLEAR.
4. Complete the practice examples of RESTORE.
5. Complete the self-test data file.

Storing information to be available for later use is one of the greatest advantages of the microcomputer. This chapter will demonstrate how to use stored DATA again and again. First, a short review of the DATA and READ commands: Remember, the DATA line can be placed anywhere in the program, and the READ command can be used to assign labels to items in a DATA line.

Figure 19-1
The OD error message is given when the RESTORE command is misplaced or when you ask the microcomputer to look for more items than there are in a DATA line. The OD message is most often a signal that the programmer has omitted a DATA line.

Definitions

• **RESTORE:** The RESTORE command tells the computer to return the first DATA statement in the program. Failure to include this will get an "OUT OF DATA" error. The computer will read the DATA statements in the order that they appear and move automatically to the next item until all stored values have been used. To get the computer to reread the list, it is necessary to include a RESTORE command.

• **OD error:** There are no data in the data file.

• **CLEAR:** Reserves space in RAM and sets all numeric variables to zero and string variables to null.

===================== **QUESTIONS AND ANSWERS** =====================

QUESTION   What does the RESTORE command do?

ANSWER   The RESTORE command instructs the micro-
                computer to replace used data. Remember, the

READ command takes data from the microcomputer's memory. The RESTORE command allows data to be used and reused.

QUESTION   When should the RESTORE command be used?

ANSWER   Whenever a program is written that calls for more than one use of the data.

QUESTION   Does it matter where the RESTORE command is placed?

ANSWER   Yes; it must be used within the limits of the loop that return the program to read the data.

QUESTION   Why is the CLEAR command needed?

ANSWER   To provide a site in the microcomputer's memory to place string variables when working with data lines. If the CLEAR command is not used, only a limited space is provided for such use.

QUESTION   What does the CLEAR command do?

ANSWER   CLEAR instructs designated locations in the microcomputer's memory to be used for working with string variables. CLEAR returns number variables to zero and text or string variables to no value.

QUESTION   Can text or string variables be manipulated without the CLEAR command?

ANSWER   Yes, if the use is held to a small number of characters, usually 200 or less.

Set up a file, use it, and replace it.

```
Command:  5 PRINT "STUDENTS' NAMES"
         10 DATA JOE,SUE,MAT
         20 FOR Y = 1 TO 3
         25 READ A$
         30 PRINT A$
         35 NEXT
```

Example 19-1

Command: RUN

Result: **See it on the screen like this:**
STUDENTS' NAMES
JOE
SUE
MAT

> It works. Ok, enough review; let's work on the RESTORE idea.
>
> Add line 40 to your program.

Command: 40 GOTO 10

Command: RUN

Result: **The program will print out as before and stop with an out of data error message.**
STUDENTS' NAMES
JOE
SUE
MAT
??OD ERROR??

> OD means there are no data in the data line.
>
> Now add a RESTORE command to the program.

Command: **Type line** 37 RESTORE

```
5 PRINT "STUDENTS' NAMES"
10 DATA JOE,SUE,MAT
20 FOR Y = 1 TO 3
25 READ A$
30 PRINT A$
35 NEXT
37 RESTORE
40 GOTO 10
```

Run the program.

Results: **The program will repeat over and over the names** JOE, SUE, MAT

Command: **Use the** BREAK **function to get the program out of its loop**

> Now you know how to use data from a file and put the data back, obviously a tremendous advantage when solving problems that will use the same information again and again.

Example 19-1 *(Continued)*

Command: Let's move the RESTORE command to see where it must be to
           be effective

           Type 37 and press enter; this removes line 37 from the program

Command: Type line 9 RESTORE and enter this line

Command: RUN

Result: STUDENTS' NAMES
           JOE
           SUE
           MAT
           ??OD ERROR??

                          The RESTORE command has been placed out of
                          the reach of the GOTO loop. You can put the
                          RESTORE command back on line 37 or
                          change the GOTO to GOTO 9.

Command: 40 GOTO 9

           5 PRINT 'STUDENTS' NAMES'
           9 RESTORE
           10 DATA JOE,SUE,MAT
           20 FOR Y = 1 TO 3
           25 READ A$
           30 PRINT A$
           35 NEXT
           40 GOTO 9

Result: RUN the program; it works just as when the RESTORE
           command was on line 37. Remember to keep the RESTORE
           command within the loop used to go back to the DATA line.

Example 19-1   *(Continued)*

========================= **PRACTICE EXAMPLES** =========================

Type and run the following.

Command: 5 DATA 88,95,45
           10 READ A,B,C.
           15 PRINT 'STUDENT'S NAME?':INPUT A$

Example 19-2

```
20 IF A$ = "JOE" THEN PRINT "TEST SCORE FOR JOE WAS " A
30 IF A$ = "SUE" THEN PRINT "TEST SCORE FOR SUE WAS " B
40 IF A$ = "MAT" THEN PRINT "TEST SCORE FOR MAT WAS " C
45 RESTORE
60 GOTO 10
```

Command: RUN

Result: STUDENT'S NAME?

Command: **Type and enter** JOE

Result: TEST SCORE FOR JOE WAS 88
STUDENT'S NAME

Command: **Type and enter** SUE

Result: TEST SCORE FOR SUE WAS 95
STUDENT'S NAME?

Command: **Use the** **BREAK** **key to interrupt the program**

> The READ statement tells the microcomputer to
> remember the DATA in terms of the variables
> A, B, or C.

Command: **Now type and enter a name not on the list; the microcomputer
does not recognize this set of characters and repeats its request.**

Result: STUDENT'S NAME

> **Try different variations to learn using a file; then
> erase for the next program.**

Example 19-2 *(Continued)*

Let's try It another way.

Command: 3 DATA "JOE",88
4 DATA "SUE",95
5 DATA "MAT",45
8 PRINT "STUDENT NAME---GRADE"
10 FOR T = 1 TO 3
15 READ A$,B
20 PRINT A$,B:NEXT

Command: RUN

Example 19-3

> **Result:**   **The following table is created:**
>
> ```
> STUDENT NAME---GRADE
> JOE              88
> SUE              95
> MAT              45
> ```
>
> > Try a short table using your ideas for a data line.
> > You can see how easy it is to put your ideas into
> > a short useful program.

Example 19-3   *(Continued)*

AGRICULTURAL EXAMPLES

Type and run the following program:

```
10 PRINT "HAY"
20 PRINT "THIS PROGRAM WILL TEST YOUR KNOWLEDGE OF HAY CROPS."
30 PRINT "WOULD YOU LIKE TO CONTINUE?"
40 PRINT "ENTER YES' OR NO'; PRESS RETURN"
50 INPUT I$
60 IF I$ <>"YES" THEN 350
65 DATA ALFALFA,CLOVER,ORCHARDGRASS,FESCUE
70 PRINT "THE BEST ALL-ROUND LEGUME HAY IS?"
75 PRINT "TYPE IN THE CORRECT ANSWER; PRESS RETURN"
80 PRINT "THE CHOICES ARE---"
85 READ A$,B$,C$,D$
90 FOR L = 1 TO 4
100 NEXT
110 PRINT A$
115 PRINT B$
120 PRINT C$
125 PRINT D$
140 RESTORE
150 INPUT E$
160 PRINT "WHICH OF THE FOUR FORAGES MAKES FOR
    AN UNBEATABLE COMBINATION?"
170 PRINT "ENTER BEST TWO ANSWERS; PRESS RETURN"
180 INPUT F$
190 PRINT "WHICH FORAGE HAS THE LOWEST FEED VALUE BUT MAKES
    A GOOD PASTURE FOR CATTLE?"
200 PRINT "ENTER ANSWER; PRESS RETURN"
210 INPUT G$
```

Example 19-4

```
220 PRINT "THE CORRECT ANSWERS ARE"
230 READ A$,B$,C$,D$
240 FOR L = 1 TO 3
250 NEXT L
260 PRINT A$
270 PRINT A$ " AND " C$
280 PRINT D$
300 PRINT "YOUR ANSWERS WERE:"
310 PRINT E$
320 PRINT F$
330 PRINT G$
340 END
350 PRINT "SORRY YOU FEEL THAT WAY."
500 END
520 FOR T = 1 TO 500
530 NEXT T
540 RETURN
```

Example 19-4 *(Continued)*

Type and run the following program:

```
5 PRINT "LITTER SIZE AND MARKET WEIGHT"
10 DATA PAT,42,10,2455
12 DATA SUE,06,8,1915
14 DATA LIZ,14,11,2365
50 PRINT "WHICH OF THE FOLLOWING ITEMS DO YOU WANT TO VIEW
   (ENTER 1,2,OR 3)?"
53 RESTORE
55 PRINT "1. SOW ID'S & AGE IN MOS"
57 PRINT "2. MARKET WEIGHT OF SOW LITTERS"
58 PRINT "3. LITTER SIZE BY SOW"
60 PRINT "4. ENTER 4 TO END THIS PROGRAM"
65 INPUT X
70 IF X = 1 THEN 100
75 IF X = 2 THE 200
80 IF X = 3 THEN 300
85 IF X = $ THEN 1000
90 END
100 PRINT "SOW ID & AGE IN MOS"
110 FOR X = 1 TO 3
115 READ A$,B,C,D
120 PRINT A$,B
125 NEXT
130 FOR A = 1 TO 1000:NEXT
132 CLS
135 GOTO 50
```

Example 19-5

```
200   PRINT "MARKET WEIGHT OF SOW LITTERS"
210 FOR X = 1 TO 3
215 READ A$,B,C,D
220 PRINT A$,D
225 NEXT
230 FOR A = 1 TO 1000:NEXT
232 CLS
235 GOTO 50
300 PRINT "LITTER SIZE BY SOW"
310 FOR X = 1 TO 3
315 READ A$,B,C,D
320 PRINT A$,C
325 NEXT
330 FOR A = 1 TO 1000:NEXT
332 CLS
335 GOTO 50
1000 PRINT "      -----THE END-----"
1010 END
```

Example 19-5 *(Continued)*

=============== **SELF-TEST EXAMPLE** ===============

1 Using the following data,

> JONES 511 gets $4.75 per hour
> SMITH 611 gets $5.10 per hour
> BROWN 711 gets $9.00 per hour

set up a DATA file with three options:

1. Option one prints only the names of workers
2. Option two prints name and ID
3. Option three prints name, ID, and salary

SUMMARY

In this chapter you have learned how information stored as DATA can be used over and over. The reuse of DATA can best occur when RESTORE has been included in the program.

20

DIM Is a DIMension

In this chapter we define and discuss the reason for the DIM command. The conditions under which the DIM will function are also reviewed.

Objectives

1. Learn the function of DIMension.
2. Complete the practice examples of the DIM.
3. Complete the self-test using the DIM.

The DIM command allows a program to label a large amount of information (variables). Labeled variables are stored in an array. An array is stored-related variables.

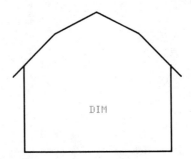

Figure 20-1
DIM groups related variables under one variable
name and reserves space in memory for the items in
that array.

Definitions

• **DIM:** The DIM command is used in conjunction with an array or matrix of variables. This provides an opportunity for the programmer to use a variable name with subscripts. The array is a way to identify a sequence of related numbers. A table of numbers is visualized by the computer as an array. The individual numbers within a table are elements in an array.

• **Array:** The storage of data with the use of a subscripted variable.

═════════════════ **QUESTIONS AND ANSWERS** ═════════════════

QUESTION	When should the DIM command be used in a program?
ANSWER	Any time a subscript in a subscripted variable is more than ten you must use a DIMension command.
QUESTION	In what form is the DIM written?
ANSWER	Line number DIM variable (number)
QUESTION	What is an array?
ANSWER	An array is a list of related variables. Items in an array are labeled variables.

QUESTION   Is an ARRAY a command?

ANSWER   No, the ARRAY is simply a way to store large amounts of information under a single variable name.

QUESTION   Must a DIM command be used with an ARRAY?

ANSWER   No, you do not have to use a DIM command if the number of items in the array is lower than 11.

=================== **PRACTICE EXAMPLES** ===================

Type the following program.

```
Command:  10 PRINT 'BUSHELS OF CORN BY FIELD'.
          20 DATA 95,85,99,100,98
          30 FOR x = 1 TO 5
          40 READ A
          50 PRINT A
          60 NEXT

Run the program. Here are the results:

          BUSHELS OF CORN BY FIELD
          95
          85
          99
          100
          98
```

Example 20-1

Now let's try a DIM command. Type and run the following program.

```
Command:  10 PRINT 'BUSHELS OF CORN BY FIELD'
          20 DATA 95,85,99,100,98
          30 DIM A(5)
          35 FOR X = 1 TO 5
          40 READ A(5)
```

Example 20-2

```
50 PRINT A(5)
60 NEXT
```

Here are the results:

```
BUSHELS OF CORN BY FIELD
95
85
99
100
98
```

Example 20-2 *(Continued)*

Let's try another DIM example. Type the following program.

```
Command: 10 PRINT "PRODUCTION"
         20 PRINT "BUSHELS OF CORN"
         30 DATA 100,200,150,160,180,100,110,200,100,120,130,150
         40 DATA 90,80,100,120,130,140,160,100,85,95,90,110
         50 PRINT "PROD YR1","PROD YR2"
         60 DIM A(12),B(12)
         70 FOR X = 1 TO 12
         80 READ (X)
         90 NEXT
         100 FOR X = 1 TO 12
         110 READ B(X)
         120 NEXT
         130 X=0
         140 X=X+1
         145 IF X=13 THEN END
         150 PRINT A(X),B(X)
         160 GOTO 140
```

Run the program. The results will look like this:

```
PRODUCTION
BUSHELS OF CORN
PROD YR1                    PROD YR2
100                         90
200                         80
150                         100
160                         120
180                         130
100                         140
110                         160
200                         100
```

Example 20-3

100	85
120	95
130	90
150	110

Example 20-3   *(Continued)*

Here are some other practical examples. Type and run the following program.

```
5 REM STOCK
6 PRINT "STOCK AVAILABLE"
7 PRINT "DIMINISHING BALANCE ON HAND AND ORDER SYSTEM"
20 DATA HACKSAW,HS BLADE,B RULE,M SNIP,FILE,C CHISEL
30 DATA C PUNCH,PLIERS,SC AWL,C SQUARE,BP HAMMER,WO MALLET
32 DATA 12,48,12,6,36,30
34 DATA 12,8,4,3,6,4
40 PRINT "ITEM","NUMBER"
45 DIM A$(12),B(12)
50 FOR X = 1 TO 12
60 READ A$(X)
70 NEXT
100 FOR X = 1 TO 12
110 READ B(X)
115 PRINT X;A$(X),B(X)
120 NEXT
145 IF X=13 THEN 170
150 PRINT X;A$,B
160 GOTO 120
170 PRINT "DO YOU WANT TO CHANGE THE NUMBER OF INVENTORY ITEMS?"
175 INPUT R$
180 IF R$="NO" THEN PRINT "THEN YOUR INVENTORY REMAINS THE SAME.
    THE END":END
190 CLS
300 X=0
302 X=X+1
303 IF X=13 THEN 400
305 PRINT "HOW MANY "A$(X)"'S DID YOU SELL TODAY?"
310 INPUT N
312 B(X)=B(X)-N
340 GOTO 302
400 CLS
410 PRINT "YOUR PRESENT STOCK LEVEL IS"
411 PRINT "ITEM","NUMBER"
412 X=0
413 X=X+1
```

Example 20-4

```
415 IF X = 13 THEN END
420 PRINT X;A$(X),B(X)
430 GOTO 413
```

Example 20-4 (Continued)

Type and run the following program (SAVE this program for use in Chapter 22).

```
10 PRINT "B & I EQUIPMENT SALES"
20 PRINT "RECORD OF TRACTORS SOLD DURING LAST FISCAL YEAR"
30 DATA 125,228,245,247,252,301,306,308,310,311
50 DATA 12000,28000,35000,14000,12500,60000,35000,45000,
   15000,15500
70 DATA 8000,20000,32000,10000,10300,58000,33000,42000,
   11000,13500
90 DIM A(10),B(10),C(10),D(10)
100 FOR X = 1 TO 10
110 READ A(X)
120 NEXT
130 FOR X = 1 TO 10
140 READ B(X)
150 NEXT
160 FOR X = 1 TO 10
170 READ C(X)
180 NEXT
190 PRINT "EQUIP-PRICE-COST-PROFIT"
200 X=0
210 X=X+1
220 IF X = 11 THEN 270
230 D(X)=B(X)-C(X)
240 PRINT A(X);B(X);C(X);D(X)
245 FOR T = 1 TO 500:NEXT
250 GOTO 210
270 END
```

The results will be:

```
B&I EQUIPMENT SALES
RECORD OF TRACTORS SOLD FOR LAST FISCAL YEAR
EQU#        PRICE       COST        PROFIT
125         12000       8000        4000
228         28000       20000       8000
245         35000       32000       3000
247         14000       10000       4000
252         12500       10300       2200
301         60000       58000       2000
```

Example 20-5

```
306        35000        33000        2000
308        45000        42000        3000
310        15000        11000        4000
311        15500        13500        2000
```

Example 20-5   *(Continued)*

════════════════════════ **SELF-TEST EXAMPLES** ════════════════════════

1 Develop a program using a DIM command to set up a table in the following form:

MILK PRODUCTION
COW-AGE-PRODUCTION

1	2	18000
2	8	20000
3	7	17000
4	5	15000
5	4	16000
6	5	21000
7	4	17000

2 Prepare a program using a DIM A$(12) to produce this list:

TOOLS IN STOCK

1 HACKSAW
2 HACKSAW BLADES
3 BENCH RULE
4 METAL SNIPS
5 FILE
6 COLD CHISEL
7 CENTER PUNCH
8 PLIERS
9 SCRATCH AWL
10 COMB SQUARE

11 B.P. HAMMER
12 WOODEN MALLET

SUMMARY

Space in the microcomputer's memory is reserved when DIM is appropriately used with subscript variables. The practice examples have provided practical applications of the DIMension command.

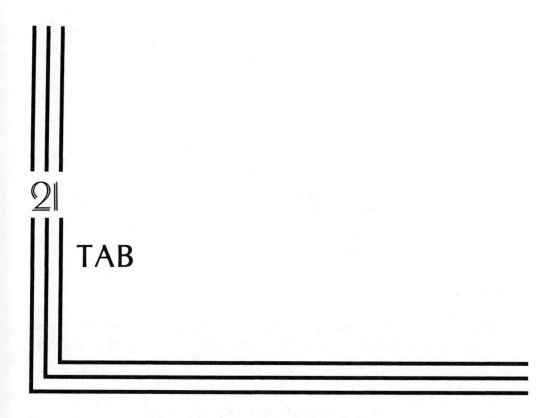

21

TAB

The microcomputer BASIC language contains a TAB command that allows information to be printed at various locations on the screen or printout. A simplified version of TAB is presented in this chapter.

Objectives

1. Determine the function of TAB.
2. Complete the practice examples of TAB.
3. Complete the TAB self-test.

The TAB is used in the placement of information, symbols, or graphics. TAB in the computer functions much like tab on the typewriter. This command sends the pointer to the column immediately following the number specified in the TAB command, and the microcomputer starts printing.

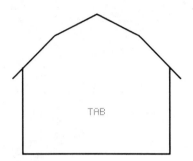

Figure 21-1
The TAB function is used to arrange the desired positioning of information when a program is executed.

Definition

• **TAB:** TAB directs the microcomputer to a specific column location. The command TAB is used prior to a printer operation command.

═══════════════ **QUESTIONS AND ANSWERS** ═══════════════

QUESTION   What is the function of TAB?

ANSWER   The TAB function is like the TAB on a typewriter. It commands the microcomputer to print at the next column following the number specified in the TAB command.

QUESTION   How do you write a TAB command?

ANSWER   Type line number TAB(column number)

QUESTION   How useful is TAB?

ANSWER   TAB can be used to space output information and display graphic information.

═══════════════ **PRACTICE EXAMPLES** ═══════════════

Type and run the following program.

TAB   **179**

```
Command:   5 REM BUSHELS
           10 PRINT "BUSHELS OF CORN BY FIELD"
           20 DATA 95,85,99,100,98
           30 FOR X = 1 TO 5
           40 READ A
           50 PRINT A
           60 NEXT

Result:    BUSHELS OF CORN BY FIELD
           98
           85
           99
           100
           98
```

Example 21-1

Now let's add a TAB command:

```
Command:   5 REM BUSHELS
           10 PRINT TAB(3)"BUSHELS OF CORN BY FIELD"
           20 DATA 95,85,99,100,98
           30 FOR X = 1 TO 5
           40 READ A
           50 PRINT TAB(12)A
           60 NEXT

Results    (see how the numbers have been indented):
           BUSHELS OF CORN BY FIELD
                      95
                      85
                      99
                      100
                      98
```

Example 21-2

Type and run this program without the TAB( ) and then add the TAB to see the results.

```
10 DIM A$(12)
20 DATA HACKSAW,HACKSAW BLADES,BENCH RULE,METAL SNIPS,FILE,COLD CHISEL
30 DATA CENTER PUNCH,PLIERS,SCRATCH AWL,COMB SQUARE,B.P. HAMMER,
   WOODEN MALLET
35 PRINT TAB(8) "TOOLS IN STOCK"
40 FOR X = 1 TO 12
50 READ A$(X)
60 PRINT TAB(8)X;A$(X)
70 NEXT
```

Results:

```
TOOLS IN STOCK
1 HACKSAW
2 HACKSAW BLADES
3 BENCH RULE
4 METAL SNIPS
5 FILE
6 COLD CHISEL
7 CENTER PUNCH
8 PLIERS
9 SCRATCH AWL
10 COMB SQUARE
11 B.P. HAMMER
12 WOODEN MALLET
```

Example 21-3

Type and run the following program:

```
Command:  10 PRINT TAB(5) "PRODUCTION"
          20 PRINT TAB(3) "BUSHELS OF CORN"
          30 DATA 100,200,150,160,180,100,110,200,100,120,130,150
          40 DATA 90,80,100,120,130,140,160,100,85,95,90,110
          50 PRINT "PROD YR1","PROD YR2"
          60 DIM A(12),B(12)
          70 FOR X = 1 TO 12
          80 READ A(X)
          90 NEXT
          100 FOR X = 1 TO 12
          110 READ B(X)
          120 NEXT
          130 X=0
          140 X=X+1
          145 IF X=13 THEN END
          150 PRINT A(X),B(X)
          160 GOTO 140
```

Example 21-4

TAB   **181**

Result: The program title is evenly spaced on the screen:

```
            PRODUCTION
          BUSHELS OF CORN
     PROD YR1          PROD YR2
     100                90
     200                80
     150                100
     160                120
     180                130
     100                140
     110                160
     200                100
     100                85
     120                95
     130                90
     150                110
```

Example 21-4   *(Continued)*

=============================== **SELF-TEST EXAMPLE** ===============================

1 Use the TAB command to center the following PRINT
statements on the screen:

line 1	WELCOME
line 2	AGRICULTURAL SOCIETY
line 3	1990

SUMMARY

TAB is used with the PRINT command. The function of TAB in the
microcomputer is similar to tab on a typewriter. The appearance
of information on the screen or printout is greatly enhanced by a
more esthetic positioning.

22

ON GOTO . . . ON GOSUB

This chapter reviews the function of the GOTO and GOSUB commands. Explanation of how the ON GOTO can be used to replace several IF . . . THEN commands is discussed. A practical application of the ON GOSUB is illustrated.

Objectives

1. Learn the function of ON GOTO.
2. Learn the function of ON GOSUB.
3. Complete the practice examples of ON GOTO and ON GOSUB.
4. Complete the ON GOSUB self-test.

The ON GOTO and ON GOSUB are expanded capabilities of the GOTO and GOSUB. The GOTO command allows the program to send the microcomputer to a line out of numerical order. The GOSUB command is a specialized form of the GOTO command.

The GOSUB command remembers where it came from, completes its task, when a RETURN command is included, and returns to the next line in the program immediately following the GOSUB statement from which it came. ON GOSUB and ON GOTO are variants of the IF . . . THEN command. A one-line command may be needed when using the ON command rather than several IF . . . THEN command lines.

Figure 22-1
The ON GOTO and ON GOSUB commands extend the capability of producing a more efficient program when several options are within a single program.

Definitions

● **ON GOTO:** The ON GOTO provides an opportunity for the programmer to send the microcomputer to one of several lines in a program, to execute that series of line commands, and then to end the program.

● **ON GOSUB:** The ON GOSUB provides an opportunity for the programmer to go to one of several different subroutines and with a RETURN to go to the next line in the program.

========= **QUESTIONS AND ANSWERS** ========

QUESTION   Is the ON GOTO a subroutine?

ANSWER   No, the ON GOTO simply sends the micro-computer to another line number.

QUESTION   Can ON GOTO be used without a RETURN?

ANSWER   Yes, but an END statement must be incorporated into the sequences of lines to which the ON GOTO is directed.

QUESTION   What happens when the input or value is incorrect or false?

ANSWER   The microcomputer uses the same decision-making capability as with the IF . . . THEN. If the value is greater or less than, the microcomputer ignores the instruction and moves to the next line of the program.

QUESTION   Can ON GOSUB be used without a RETURN?

ANSWER   No; the RETURN statement must be developed to return the program to its normal conclusion.

QUESTION   How is the ON GOSUB different from the GOTO?

ANSWER   The ON GOSUB under specific conditions identified after the ON statement will direct the program to a series of subroutines.

QUESTION   How does the ON GOSUB differ from the IF . . . THEN statement?

ANSWER   All that can be done in the ON GOSUB command can be achieved with the proper sequencing of the IF . . . THEN command.

QUESTION   What is the advantage of ON GOSUB over the IF . . . THEN?

ANSWER   The ON GOSUB can achieve in one line what it would take one or more IF . . . THEN commands to achieve. The ON GOSUB allows the programmer to choose from a list of line numbers to go to.

The use of the ON GOTO is designed to allow the programmer to route the operator to any one of several options.

PRACTICE EXAMPLES

Type and run the following program:

```
Command:  5 REM ON GOTO 1
          20 PRINT "SELECT A NUMBER 1,2, OR 3."
          30 INPUT A
          40 ON A GOTO 100,200,300
          100 PRINT "YOU SELECTED 1"
          110 END
          200 PRINT "YOU SELECTED 2"
          210 END
          300 PRINT "YOU SELECTED 3"
          310 END

READY.
```

Example 22-1

The preceding program allows for the selection of three options. It should be noted that at the end of each of the GOTO statements there is an END statement, lines 110, 210, and 310. This is the main difference between ON GOTO and ON GOSUB.

Try this program:

```
Command:  5 REM ON GOSUB 1
          10 PRINT "SELECT A NUMBER FROM 1,2 OR 3"
          20 INPUT A
          30 ON A GOSUB 100,200,300
          40 GOTO 10
          100 PRINT "YOU SELECTED 1"
          110 RETURN
          200 PRINT "2 IS AN EXCELLENT SELECTION"
          210 RETURN
          300 PRINT "YOU CHOOSE 3! GOOD"
          310 RETURN

READY.
```

Example 22-2

The illustration on ON GOSUB will take you to one of the three selected GOSUBs and then RETURN. The program can then be completed in a normal manner.

For a practical application of the ON GOSUB, try this
exercise:

```
5  PRINT TAB(6)"'STOCK ON HAND'"
10 PRINT TAB(3)"BALANCE AND ORDER SYSTEM"
15 GOSUB 1000
18 PRINT "STOCK IS LISTED BY ITEM NO., ITEM & NO. OF EACH ITEM."
20 DATA HACKSAW,H.S.BLADES,BENCH RULE,METAL SNIPS,FILE,COLD CHISEL
30 DATA CENTER PUNCH,PLIERS,SCRATCH AWL,COMB,SQUARE,B.P. HAMMER,
   WOOD MALLET
32 DATA 12,48,12,6,36,30
34 DATA 12,8,4,3,6,4
40 PRINT "ITEM","NUMBER"
45 DIM A$(12),B(12)
50 FOR X= 1 TO 12
60 READ A$(X)
70 NEXT
100 FOR X= 1 TO 12
110 READ B(X)
120 NEXT
125 X=0
128 X= X+1
145 IF X = 13 THEN 165
150 PRINTX;A$(X),B(X)
160 GOTO 128
165 FOR T = 1 TO 2000:NEXT
168 CLS
170 INPUT"DO YOU WANT TO CHANGE THE NUMBER OF INVENTORY ITEMS";R$
180 IF R$="NO" THEN 1500
300 X=0
302 X=X+1
303 IF X=13 THEN 410
305 PRINT"HOW MANY "A$(X)"'S DID YOU SELL?"
310 INPUT N
312 B(X)=B(X)-N
340 GOTO 302
410 PRINT"YOUR PRESENT STOCK LEVEL IS "
411 PRINT"ITEM","NUMBER"
412 X=0
413 X=X+1
415 IF X = 13 THEN 432
420 PRINTX;A$(X),B(X)
430 GOTO 413
432 FOR T = 1 TO 2000:NEXT
433 CLS
435 PRINT TAB(3) "'SOURCE OF STOCK'"
440 PRINT"PRESS NUMBER 1,2,OR 3 TO DETERMINE WHERE TO ORDER ITEMS"
450 PRINT TAB(5)"(1) ITEMS 1 TO 4 "
```

Example 22-3

```
455 PRINT TAB(5)"(2) ITEMS 4 TO 8"
460 PRINT TAB(5)"(3) ITEMS 9 TO 12"465 PRINT "(ENTER '5'
    TO END THE PROGRAM)"
470 INPUT Z
474 IF Z = 5 THEN 1510
475 PRINT "ORDER THESE ITEMS:"
480 ON Z GO TO 500,600,700
494 GOSUB 1000
495 CLS
496 GOTO 435
500 PRINT TAB(2)"HACKSAW"
505 PRINT TAB(2)"H.S. BLADES"
510 PRINT TAB(2)"BENCH RULE"
515 PRINT TAB(2)"MET SNIPS"
518 PRINT TAB(12) "FROM"
520 PRINT TAB(7)"SMITH SUPPLY INC"
525 PRINT TAB(7)"2345 S.W. AVE"
530 PRINT TAB(7)"ST. LOUIS, MO. 62903"
535 PRINT TAB(7)"ATTN. BILL SMITH"
540 PRINT TAB(7)"PH. 503-555-7349"
594 GOSUB 1000
595 CLS
596 GOTO 435
600 PRINT TAB(2)"FILE"
605 PRINT TAB(2)"COLD CHISEL"
610 PRINT TAB(2)"CENTER PUNCH"
615 PRINT TAB(2)"PLIERS"
617 PRINT TAB(12)"FROM"
620 PRINT TAB(7)"T&T DIST. CO."
625 PRINT TAB(7)"1100 EAST AVE."
630 PRINT TAB(7)"CHICAGO, IL. 247"
640 PRINT TAB(7)"PH. 500-600-8000
694 GOSUB 1000
695 CLS
696 GOTO 435
700 PRINT TAB(2)"SCRATCH AWL"
705 PRINT TAB(2)"COMB. SQUARE"
710 PRINT TAB(2)"B.P. HAMMER"
715 PRINT TAB(2)"WOOD MALLET"
717 PRINT TAB(12)"FROM"
720 PRINT TAB(7)"COS SUPPLY CO."
730 PRINT TAB(7)"3434 DRIVE AVE"
740 PRINT TAB(7)"DALLAS, TX"
750 PRINT TAB(7)"PH. 987-653-4210"
755 GOSUB 1000
760 CLS
770 GOTO 435
1000 FOR T = 1 TO 1500:NEXT
1020 CLS
1030 RETURN
```

Example 22-3 (Continued)

```
1500 PRINT "THEN YOUR INVENTORY REMAINS THE SAME"
1510 PRINT TAB(10)"THE END"
1520 END
```

Example 22-3 *(Continued)*

════════ SELF-TEST EXAMPLE ════════

1 Use the ON GOSUB command to add the following information to the "B&I EQUIPMENT SALES" program. (The B&I equipment sales program is given in Chapter 20.)

Equipment 125, 228, 245 should be ordered from:

TC Equipment Dealer
2500 5th St.
Rockfort, OH 61522

Equipment 247, 252, 301 should be ordered from:

Bob White Wholesale
35 4th St.
Cleveland, IN 32141

Equipment 306, 308, 310, 311 should be ordered from:

Tractor Supply Co.
1385 N. Clay St.
Tampa, GA 23566

SUMMARY ════════════════════════

The ON GOTO and ON GOSUB command the microprocessor to select from several alternatives in completing a program. The ON GOTO and ON GOSUB are effective in reducing the need for several IF . . . THEN commands.

23

Spread Sheet Operations

Now that you have completed an introduction to BASIC programming and are familiar with microcomputer machine operations, familiarity with one of the most widely used software packages is next.

Most microcomputer manufacturers have a *spread sheet* program available for business use. Examples of these programs are VisiCalc® for Apple, SPECTACULATOR for TRS-80 color computers, and EASYCALC for Commodore microcomputers. A spread sheet is a type of accounting program that offers the agriculture user flexibility in solving and performing record-keeping and forecasting problems. A spread sheet is a large electronic ledger that stores and processes information.

Objectives

1. Provide a description of the common elements of a spread sheet.

2. Illustrate farm, ranch, and agribusiness applications of a spread sheet.

SPREAD SHEET
ROWS AND COLUMNS
COORDINATES
ENTER VALUES OR LABELS
CURSOR MOVEMENT
COORDINATE ENTRIES

Figure 23-1
An understanding of spread sheet cursor movement, the coordinate concept, and how to enter values or labels in rows and columns will provide a framework for solving agricultural problems with spread sheets.

Definitions

• **Spread sheet:** A large tablelike organization of rows and columns that provides places to enter information. A spread sheet (Table 23-1) may have as many as 60 columns and 250 plus rows.

Table 23-1

	COLUMNS							
	A	B	C	D	E	F	G	H
Rows 1								
2								
3								
4								
5								
6								
7								
8								
9								
10								

● **Rows and columns:** Rows are the horizontal layers of numbers or symbols that are placed on a spread sheet. In Table 23-2, row 1 contains the titles of each column, while row 2 contains all the grade information about the student JOE.

Columns are the vertical lists of numbers or symbols that are placed on a spread sheet. In Table 23-2, column A contains the title of the column and all the students' names, column D contains the title of column D and the list of average grades.

Table 23-2

	COLUMN A	COLUMN B	COLUMN C	COLUMN D
Row 1	Name	Quiz	Exam	Average
Row 2	JOE	80	90	86
Row 3	MARY	60	100	84
Row 4	PETE	90	100	96
Row 5	LISA	100	90	94

● **Coordinates:** An identification that locates one spot on the spread sheet. A spread sheet coordinate is identified by listing the column location and then the row location. For example, coordinate B2 is the student JOE'S quiz grade, 80. The word average is located at coordinate D1.

● **Entered values or labels:** Information entered at spread sheet coordinates is recognized as having either number identity or symbol identity. Number- or value-identified information can be used in computation. If information is not intended to be analyzed mathematically, it is identified as being a label. See specific machine instructions concerning how to store values or labels at spread sheet coordinates.

In Table 23-2, all the words in column A and the words in row 1 were entered on the spread sheet as labels. All the numbers were entered as values. When entered as values, they can be manipulated in math operations. If you are entering a number that will later be added, be sure to enter it as a value. Since coordinate values will later be identified as, for example, B2, it is important to indicate whether B2 is to be handled as a label or as a value. In the example, B2 is the quiz score of the student JOE. Later at coordinate D2 the quiz score will be computed. The spread sheet program will recognize B2 as a value when one of several math operations symbols precedes the entering of B2. The plus (+) sign is frequently used to designate B2 as a value, +B2.

• **Cursor movement:** Once the spread sheet program is loaded into the microcomputer, the cursor will appear. Information as labels or values can be entered at the site of the cursor. The cursor can be easily moved from coordinate to adjacent coordinate or to a distant coordinate. Refer to instructions for the spread sheet program for specific details on cursor movement. For Apple programs, use the > (more than) key, followed by the coordinate of the wanted cursor site.

• **Coordinate entries:** Spread sheet entries can be made at the coordinate site when the cursor is at the coordinate where the entry is to be placed. Refer to the spread sheet program instructions and follow the directions for cursor movement. Coordinate entries are generally limited to a maximum of nine characters. There are program modifications that can be used to alter the number of characters listed at each coordinate.

• **Coordinate formulas:** The power of spread sheet analysis is in its ability to compute coordinate entries that are based on the values entered at other coordinate sites. In Table 23-3, student grades are derived from the quiz and exam scores. This means that when a score is changed the student grade is automatically recalculated. Further power of the spread sheet will be examined when coordinate formula replication is discussed. In Table 23-3, the quiz score represents 40 percent of the final grade, while the exam score contributes 60 percent to a final grade. Following the example of JOE, the quiz score of 80 was entered at site B2 and an exam score of 90 was entered at coordinate C2.

Table 23-3
Sample Entries

	A	B	C	D
		Quiz	Exam	Average
1	Name	Quiz	Exam	Average
2	JOE	80	90	enter (B2*.4)+(C2*.6)
3	MARY	60	100	enter (B3*.4)+(C3*.6)

At coordinate D2 a value entry of B2 times 40 percent plus C2 times 60 percent was used to derive the final grade of 86 (see Table 23-4). To enter B2 as a value; a computation sign must precede the letter B. In this example, the following is the exact entry for coordinate D2: (B2*.4) + (C2*.6). The advantage of entering this formula at coordinate D2 is that, whenever a different quiz score is entered for JOE, the formula will recalculate and list the corrected final score.

Table 23-4
Sample Spread Sheet Listing

	A	B	C	D
1	Name	Quiz	Exam	Average
2	JOE	80	90	86
3	MARY	60	100	84

Remember, the spread sheet will print the results of the formula at the coordinate site where the formula was entered. Usually, the formula used to calculate a coordinate value will appear at the top of the spread sheet when the cursor is at the coordinate site.

=========== **SELF-TEST EXAMPLE** ===========

Use a spread sheet planning form (Figure 23-2) to set up the following example. Include the following column headings: Cow Name; Daily Production; Age; Actual Production; Adjusted Production (see Table 23-5).

Table 23-5

	A	B	C	D	E
1	NAME	DAY PROD	AGE	ACT PROD	ADJ PROD
2	ADA	40			
3	BOSSY				
4	GEORGE				
5	HANK				

Spread Sheet Planning Form

Columns

Rows	A	B	C	D	E	F	G
1							
2							
3							
4							
5							
6							
7							
8							
9							
10							

Columns

Rows	H	I	J	K	L	M	N
1							
2							
3							
4							
5							
6							
7							
8							
9							
10							

Figure 23-2

1 Dairy cow milk production for 305 days, age adjusted.

Cow Ada produced 40 pounds per day and is 4 years old

Cow Bossy produced 45 pounds per day and is 3 years old

Cow George produced 42 pounds per day and is 3 years old

Cow Hank produced 56 pounds per day and is 6 years old

The age adjusting factors are as follows;

1.31 for 2 year olds
1.18 for 3 year olds
1.08 for 4 year olds
No factor for 5 years or older

USING SPREAD SHEET REPLICATION FEATURES

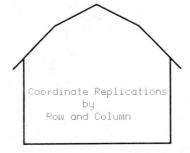

Coordinate Replications
by
Row and Column

Figure 23-3
The spread sheet program's real power is more evident when replication features have been learned. These features allow the operator to move a formula that is located at one coordinate to another coordinate or a series of other coordinates. This feature is especially useful if the operator is adjusting values for reoccurring calculations such as accumulated interest.

Student Grades Example

In the student quiz, exam, and average example (Table 23-3), column D calculated the average grade using the following formula. Sixty percent of the exam grade is added to 40 percent of the quiz grade to determine an average grade. As indicated, the formula for JOE's average is (B2*.4) + (C2*.6) and MARY's average formula is (B3*.4)+(C3*.6). The power of the replication function can be demonstrated when realizing that, if the class size were 150 students, much time would be needed to repeat or replicate the 150 formulas needed to complete column D. By using a spread sheet replication function (Table 23-6), all 150 formulas can be completed with a few commands. These commands will vary according to the spread sheet instructions but are basically as follows.

Step 1. Enter the formula or item to be repeated.

Step 2. Activate the program's replication function.

Step 3. Enter the coordinate source of the replication.

Step 4. Enter the beginning and ending coordinates where the replication is to take place.

Step 5. If necessary, indicate whether the replication is a relative or constant function (see the next example for a discussion of constant and relative replication functions).

Table 23-6
Grade Spread Sheet Example

	A	B	C	D
1	Name	Quiz	Exam	Average
2	Joe	enter actual	enter actual	enter (B2*.4)+(C2*.6)
3	Mary	data this	data this	replicate formula for
		column	column	this column

Sample Spread Sheet Layouts for Agriculture

Table 23-7
Total Income & Expenses Projection

	Item	1983	1984	1985	1986
1	Item	1983	1984	1985	1986
2	Annual Sales	40000	(B2*1.10) replicate with relative function		
3	Crop Sales	65000	(B3*1.05) replicate with relative function		
4	Total Sales	(B2+B3)	replicate with relative function		
5	Crop Expense	55000	replicate with constant function		
6	Annual Expense	29000	(B6*1.25) replicate with relative function		
7	Total Expense	(B5+B6)	replicate with relative function		
8	Net Income	(B4−B7)	replicate with relative function		

Table 23-7 shows a projection of future sales and expenses. The 1983 figures represent actual income and expense. The bases for projection are as follows. It was expected that animal sales (row 2) will increase at the rate of 10 percent per year, crop sales will increase 5 percent per year, crop expenses are expected to remain constant, and animal expenses are expected to increase 25 percent per year. This problem can most easily be solved by using the replication function. Notice that after this program has been properly entered the replication function will complete each row.

===================== **SELF-TEST EXAMPLE** =====================

1 Use a spread sheet planning form to set up the following grain storage problem. The problem is to complete Table 23-8, which includes current income and projected income for six future months. Today's date is December 1. Projections are to be made for January 1, February 1, March 1, April 1, May 1, and June 1. The crop size is 30,000 bushels. The farm's fixed storage cost for the crop is $900. The December 1 price for the crop is $2.10 per bushel. The variable cost of crop storage is 4¢ per bushel per month. The crop price is expected to increase at the rate of 3 percent per month. Use the column and row titles of Table 23-8 and complete by including the entries and formulas to be replicated. Be sure to note whether replicated rows are to be repeated with a constant function or a relative function.

Table 23-8

	A	B	C	D	E	F	G	H
		Current	Jan 1	Feb 1	Mar 1	Apr 1	May 1	June 1
1								
2	Bushels							
3	Fixed Storage							
4	Variable Storage							
5	Price per Bushel							
6	Net Return							

SUMMARY

This chapter provided a practical example of how a spread sheet could be used to organize information into a table composed of rows and columns. A spread sheet planning form was outlined with a dairy example.

The several sample crop and livestock applications provide some insight to the many possible farm and ranch uses of an electronic spread sheet.

APPENDIX A

Microcomputer Periodicals

Byte
70 Main St.
Peterborough, NH 03458

Calculators/Computers
Dymax P.O. Box 310-F
Menlo Park, CA 94025

Cload Magazine
Box 1267
Goleta, CA 93017

Compute
P.O. Box 5119
Greensboro, NC 27403

Computer World
797 Washington St.
Newton, MA 02160

Educational Computer Magazine
P.O. Box 535
Cupertino, CA 95015

Intelligent Machine Journal
345 Swett Rd.
Dept. 11
Woodside, CA 94062

Microcomputing (Kilobaud
  Microcomputing)
P.O. Box 997
Farmingdale, NY 11737

Microcomputing News
1050 Commonwealth Ave.
Boston, MA 02215

Popular Computing
P.O. Box 307
Martinsville, NJ 08836

Personal Computing
1050 Commonwealth Ave.
Boston, MA 02215

Pet User Notes
Pet User Group
P.O. Box 371
Montgomeryville, PA 18936
Apple Foundation Journal

Recreational Computing
People's Computer Company
1263 El Camino Real
Menlo Park, CA 94025

Small Business Computers
33 Watching Plaza
Montclair, NJ 07042

Softside
Subscription Service Dept.
P.O. Box 68
Milford, NH 03055

Software Digest
7620 Little River Turnpike
Suite 414
Annandale, VA 22003

TRS-80
Microcomputer News
P.O. Box 2910
Ft. Worth, TX 76113

APPENDIX B

Glossary of Computer Terms

Assembler: Software; a program that allows the computer to use letter commands. The computer will receive number instructions. An assembler allows the operator to input letter instructions that are converted to the computer's binary number format.

BASIC: An acronym for Beginners All-Purpose Symbolic Instruction Code. It is an easy-to-use language that nearly all microcomputers programmed to accept.

BASIC-in ROM: This means that the ability to use BASIC programming language has been stored in the microcomputer's ROM memory.

Baud: A measure of flow of computer information. The rate is measured in bits per second. This information will tell you the highest rate of transfer possible between two devices. Typical baud rates vary from 100 to 1500 bits per second.

Binary number system: A number system based upon the digits 0 and 1. In the binary system only zeros and ones are used in combinations that can represent an inexhaustible number of alternatives. The computer's processing uses the binary number system.

Bit: The smallest unit of computer information. In the binary system a bit is either 0 or 1, positive or negative. The computer circuit is either on or off for each bit used in a calculation or program.

Bug: Computer operator slang expression that means something is not working properly. "There is a bug in the system."

Byte: The basic unit of information in a microcomputer. Consists of 8 bits. In the binary system, 8 bits allows one byte to represent at least 128 different combinations.

Cassette recorder: A hardware device used to store information taken from a microcomputer. Since most information stored in the computer is lost when the machine is turned off, it must be stored on a cassette tape by being converted to an audio signal and then recorded on tape. Cassette storage is more time consuming than disk storage.

Character: Items that are used to communicate information. In computing there are two forms of characters. The binary form of 0 and 1 is understood by the computer. The second, composed of graphic symbols, numbers, or letters, is understood by individuals. Computing requires constant translation between these two forms of characters.

Chip: Also called a microprocessor; it is a piece of silicon, smaller than a human fingernail. It contains thousands of electronic elements and circuits that provide the computing capacity of a microcomputer.

Command: An instruction given through an input device. The microcomputer executes commands as soon as they are entered in the microprocessor.

Compiler: Software; a program that translates a high-level language like BASIC into a binary machine language. One reason for adding a compiler to a microcomputer would be to establish a quicker program completion time.

Computer: A machine that follows instruction to analyze information. The difference between a calculator and a computer is that the computer can analyze both symbols and numbers. A calculator handles numbers only.

CPU: Central Processing Unit; the central controlling element of a computer. It performs calculations and directs the processing of information by the microprocessor.

CRT: Cathode Ray Tube; we know it best as a TV screen. The microcomputer may display its results as characters, numbers, or graphs on the CRT at a rate of 960 characters per second.

Cursor: A mobile blinking indicator light on the CRT screen. It lets the operator know where the next character will appear.

Data: Information in the form of words, numbers, or other symbols.

Debug: Computer slang term used to indicate that an error is being corrected in a computer program.

Disk or disc: A magnetic coated piece of recordlike plastic material that can store computer information. The most common disk is the 5¼-inch floppy or flexible disk. Floppy disks usually store 256,000 bytes of information. Disk is the preferred spelling, but either may be used.

Disk drive: A hardware device used to store information taken from a microcomputer. The disk drive converts the magnetic charge of a disk to a series of signals. A disk will store and retrieve information more quickly than a cassette tape system. The disk is also more expensive.

DOS: Disk Operating System. A series of machine language programs that control a disk drive.

Dot matrix: A printing system that uses a sequence of printed dots to create letters and other characters.

Dump: The process of copying the information that is in the memory of one device into another device. This allows memory to be used for another function.

Editor: Software; a program that allows the computer operator to more easily add or modify instructions of a program.

Error: A mistake in communication between the microcomputer operator and a computer-language command.

Error message: A TV screen message indicating that the input command has not been understood by the microprocessor.

Execute: Term used to indicate that a microprocessor has completed a command or a program.

External storage: A hardware device used to store computer information. This device is detached from the computer (e.g., disk or tape storage).

File: A list of related information.

File name: Symbols, usually numbers or letters, used to identify a file.

Flow charting: A program guide that consists of a series of graphic blocks to indicate the proper sequence of a program.

Frequency: The rate of a microcomputer's performance. Most computer components are rated for the speed at which they can complete a task.

Graphics: Use of symbols or characters to form figures like graphs, buildings, or animals. Graphics may output on a TV screen or on paper.

Hard copy: A printed copy of a microcomputer's output. This term is used to distinguish printed output from the video image of the TV screen.

Hardware: The electronic, mechanical, or magnetic devices needed for a computer system. Minimum needs are an input device, a processing machine, and an output mechanism.

High-level language: A computer language such as BASIC, that uses common English words and expressions.

Initialize: A process performed on a new disk. This process creates tracks or marks on a new disk. Initialization must be done before a disk can be used to store data.

Input: Information entered into a computer system. Information can be entered as words, numbers, or other symbols.

Instructions: A series of signals that causes the computer to perform prescribed operations similar to command.

Interactive: A term used to describe a computer system that can respond to the user's information during the operation of a program. A personal microcomputer is an interactive system.

Interface: Refers to the ability of one system or systems component to hook up and work with a second system or systems component.

Internal storage: A memory found within computers, as opposed to external memory or storage space on cassette tapes or a floppy disc.

K or kilo: Abbreviation that represents 1024 bytes of computer memory. A microcomputer with 16K has 16 times 1024 or 16,384 bytes of memory capacity.

Language: A group of instructions that allows a programmer to communicate with the computer with the use of predetermined commands. Most microcomputers "speak" BASIC.

Line: In a microcomputer program, instructions are sequenced with line numbers. Most microcomputers can handle a maximum of 256 characters per line.

Load: The process of placing information from external storage into the memory of the microcomputers. Load is the opposite of dump.

Loop: A sequence of computer program instructions that will continue to be repeated until a preset condition is met.

Machine language: A code or series of binary numbers.

Matrix printer: A hardware component; a printer that uses the matrix dot system to print letters, numbers, and symbols.

Memory: Microprocessor circuit that provide space for internal storage of information. Microcomputers will have both RAM and ROM memory.

Microprocessor: The electronic circuit or chip. It is the "brains" of the CPU.

Modem: A hardware component that converts the computer's electric signals into high- and low-tone telephone signals. A modem allows the microcomputer's information to be transmitted by telephone.

Modulator: A hardware device that allows any TV set (monitor) to be used as the video output screen for a microcomputer.

Monitor: A TV set or CRT device that provides a video screen to view output printed messages from the microprocessor.

Output: Information, as in words, numbers, or symbols, that comes from a computer processor. Output may be seen on a screen, printed on paper, or recorded on tape or disk storage devices.

Program: A list of instructions that causes a microcomputer to perform a task. Programs are usually written in a computer language such as BASIC.

Programmer: A person who understands the meaning of the predetermined commands of a computer language. A BASIC programmer can use the BASIC language to solve problems.

ROM: Read Only Memory. ROM is a circuit of electronic instructions that was placed in the microcomputer when it was manufactured. ROM instructions cannot be erased or reprogrammed by microcomputer input.

Routine: A set of instructions that is part of a program. A routine is typically repeated several times within a program.

Run: A direct instruction to the microprocessor. This command when entered will direct the microprocessor to operate a program that has been stored in the microprocessor.

Save: A direct instruction to the microprocessor that causes information to be stored on a disk or cassette tape.

Software: The instructions or programs that the microcomputer reads or uses in order to solve problems.

Storage capacity: An indicator of the number of bytes a device can store. If a disk has 400K capacity, it can store 409,600 bytes of information.

Storage device: Usually a reference to a peripheral device that can retain computer data.

Store: Term used to describe the process of placing information into a device where it can be kept permanently, such as a cassette tape or floppy disk.

String: A list or series of letters, numbers, or symbols. A sentence is a string, or a paragraph could be a string.

Subroutine: A short set of instructions that is used for a repetitious part of a program. Perhaps the most common microcomputer subroutine is a time delay or counting subroutine that causes the microprocessor to pause for a specified period time.

Tape: A magnetic tape that can be used to store computer information. The most common tape used for the microcomputer is the cassette tape or recorder size magnetic tape.

Terminal: A peripheral device that provides input across to the microprocessor. The microcomputer terminal is usually a keyboard.

Text: Computer information other than only numbers. Letters, words, and paragraphs with or without numbers are called text.

Text editor: Software; a program that makes word editing easy. Typical functions of a text editor are to (1) add words, (2) remove words, (3) find specific words, (4) create paragraphs, and (5) lay out page margins. Many other functions are available on some text editors.

Track: Similar to the groove in a record. A floppy disk has tracks or grooves along which magnetic pulses are stored. Information is read onto or recorded on floppy disk tracks and can be read from them. This is accomplished using a metallic head with metal pads that create or sense magnetic pulses.

Variable: The name given to describe a certain symbol or set of symbols. A variable's value may change. For example, when using T to represent current air temperature, T as a symbol has a value that changes.

Video monitor: Same as *Monitor* or *CRT*.

APPENDIX C

Definitions of BASIC Language Terms

CONT The CONT command is to continue the execution of a program that has been stopped. The CONT command may be used if a program has been stopped by using the STOP key (some machines), using the BREAK key, or an END statement within the program. This command will work only if no modification has been initiated in the program.

DATA The DATA command is used to hold information that will be used to fill variables in a READ command. Any type of information may be stored if separated by commas.

DIM or **DIM NAMES$** The DIM or DIM NAMES$ (check your manual for the correct usage) command is used in conjunction with an array or matrix of variables. This provides an opportunity for the programmer to use a variable name with subscripts. The array is a way to identify a sequence of related numbers. A table of numbers is visualized by the computer as an array. The individual numbers within a table are elements in an array. The array will assign a value to each component in the array.

END The END command stops the program and tells the computer there are no further statements in the program. The END command, must, therefore, be the last statement in the BASIC program. The END statement includes a line number and the word END.

FOR

FOR . . . TO

FOR . . . NEXT The FOR command is provided to allow the programmer to use a variable as a counter. The programmer must establish the variable name, identify the starting value, limit the count, and establish the quantity to be added during each cycle.

GOSUB The GOSUB command is a specialized form of the GOTO command. The GOSUB command remembers where it came from, and when it has completed its task and when a RETURN command is included, the computer will automatically return to the next line in the program immediately following the GOSUB statement from which it came.

GOTO or **GO TO** The GOTO (there may be a space between the GO and the TO) command allows the program to send the computer to a line out of numerical order.

IF . . . THEN The IF . . . THEN command provides for the evaluation of a condition or conditions and takes different actions based on the outcome. The options following the IF command may include the expressions of variables, strings, numbers, comparison, and logical operators.

INPUT The INPUT command allows the person operating the program to put information into the computer.

INT The INT command needs no further instruction to the computer. It simply connects or returns a number to an integer.

LIST The LIST command allows the programmer to look at the lines that are currently in the computer's memory. LIST will list all the lines of the program that are in the computer's memory. If there are more than will appear on the screen, LIST will move to the end of the program. If the line needed is not present, it is possible to ask for a specific line, for example, LIST 30. If more than one line is desired, it may be requested with LIST (the line number) - (the line number).

LIST 30–50 Will display all the lines from 30 through 50. If there are more than will fit on the screen, the latter will appear on a space available basis.

LOAD " " The LOAD command may give program title: for example, Load "BEEF FEEDING"

LOAD The LOAD* command transfers the program from the storage unit (usually a tape) into the computer's memory for use or modification. The LOAD statement may be just the single word LOAD.

LOAD" ", 8 The LOAD,8 command instructs the computer to search the disk for the program title in quotation marks.

LOAD,8 The LOAD,8 command instructs the computer to load the first program on the disk.

NEW The NEW command should be executed *very carefully*. This command erases the program and variables that are currently in the memory of the computer. This command is used when the user has finished with a program and has it properly stored on tape or disk or when the program is of no further value.

NEXT The NEXT command is used to complete the loop that was initiated by the FOR command.

PRINT The PRINT command instructs the computer to print the message specified. The computer will print a message, messages, or expression, each separated with a semicolon or comma but *all* enclosed in quotation marks.

READ The READ command instructs the computer to READ the DATA values stored in the program to fill variables.

REM The REM is not a command and will not be read by the computer. The REM line is employed to make the program more useful when it is LISTED.

RESTORE The RESTORE command tells the computer to return the first DATA statement in the program. Failure to include

---

*Some computers use CLOAD in place of LOAD. The combinations, options, and functions are the same. Check the operator's manual for the correct term.

this will get an "OUT OF DATA" error. The computer will read the DATA statements in the order that they appear and move automatically to the next item until all stored values have been used. To get the computer and reread the list, it is necessary to include a RESTORE command.

RETURN The RETURN command is used in conjunction with the GOSUB command.

RUN The RUN command causes the computer to execute the program. All variables entered in the program will be cleared when a run statement is executed. The computer will begin to run the program from the lowest numbered line. RUN 70 will start at line 70 and run the program from that line until the completion of the program or until you stop the program. If there is no line 70, a RUN to state may produce a UNDEF'D STATEMENT ERROR. Secure the correct line number and specify RUN.

SAVE The SAVE* command stores the program currently in the computer's memory on tape or disk. The SAVE command may be a single word.

SAVE" " The SAVE" " command may be program-title specific. If you type SAVE "BEEF FEEDING," the computer will search for the Beef Feeding program and will store it on tape.

SAVE" ",8 The SAVE" ",8 command is storage-device specific. SAVE "BEEF FEEDING",8 will store the Beef Feeding program on the disk.

SAVE,8 The SAVE,8 command will store the first program on the computer disk. If the storage device (disk or tape) is not connected, the computer will say, DEVICE NOT PRESENT ERROR.

STOP The STOP command will halt the program being run and return the control to the user.

TAB A TAB directs the microcomputer to a specific column location. The command TAB is used prior to a printer operation command.

---

*Some computers use CSAVE in place of SAVE. The combination, options, and functions are the same. Check the operator's manual for the correct term. Some computers limit the number of letters in the program title.

APPENDIX D

Error Messages: Quick Reference

When the computer is given the incorrect command, an *error message* will result. Different computer companies and different models within the same company will use different key words, letters, or symbols to notify the programmer or the operator of the error.

Error Message	Cause
AO	File already open.
BS	Reference element outside the range limit of the DIM command.
BAD DATA	Wrong type of variable for data.
BAD SUBSCRIPT	Reference element outside the range limit of the DIM command.
CN	Unable to execute CONT command.
CAN'T CONTINUE	Unable to execute CONT command.

Error Message	*Cause*
DD	DIMensioned an array already DIMensioned.
DN	Device required was not present.
DS	Direct statement in the data file.
DEVICE NOT PRESENT	Device required was not present.
/0	Commanded to divide a number by 0.
DIVISION BY ZERO	Commanded to divide a number by 0.
EXTRA IGNORED	Too many items of data to an input statement.
FC	Out of the allowable range.
FD	Wrong type of variable for data.
FM	INPUT or OUTPUT improper.
FILE NOT FOUND	Unable to find a file.
FILE NOT OPEN	File is not OPEN.
FILE OPEN	File already open.
FORMULA TOO COMPLEX	String formula too complex.
ID	INPUT command in a direct mode.
IO	CLOAD command from a bad tape.
ILLEGAL DIRECT	INPUT command in a direct mode.
ILLEGAL QUANTITY	Out of the allowable range.
LS	String is limited.
LOAD	Problem with program being loaded.
NF	NEXT command without FOR statement.
NEXT WITHOUT FOR	NEXT command without FOR statement.
NO	File is not OPEN.
NOT INPUT FILE	INPUT or OUTPUT improper.
NOT OUTPUT FILE	INPUT or OUTPUT improper.
OD	No additional DATA to be READ.
OM	Computer is OUT OF MEMORY.
OV	Number larger than capacity.
OUT OF DATA	No additional DATA to be READ.
OUT OF MEMORY	Computer is OUT OF MEMORY.
OVERFLOW	Number larger than capacity.

Error Message	*Cause*
RG	RETURN command not previously received a GOSUB command.
REDO FROM START	Character data submitted; numeric data was expected.
REDIM'D ARRAY	DIMensioned an array already DIMensioned.
RETURN WITHOUT GOSUB	RETURN command not previously received a GOSUB command.
SN	Unable to recognize the command.
ST	String formula too complex.
STRING TOO LONG	String is limited.
SYNTAX	Unable to recognize the command.
TM	Commanded to assign numeric data to a string variable.
TYPE MISMATCH	Commanded to assign numeric data to a string variable.
UL	Commanded to GOTO or GOSUB or RUN line number nonexistent.
UNDEF'D STATE-MENT	Commanded to GOTO or GOSUB or RUN line number nonexistent.
VERIFY	Unable to verify program.

APPENDIX E

Error Messages: Explanation

The following is a listing of many error messages and narrative descriptions of the probable causes.

Error Message	Cause
BAD DATA or FD	The computer was commanded to PRINT data to a file or INPUT data from a file, using the wrong type of variable for the data.
BAD SUBSCRIPT or BS	The computer has been commanded to reference an element of an array that is outside the range limit of the DIM command. The computer may also produce this error if no DIM statement is included.
CN or CAN'T CONTINUE	The computer is unable to execute the CONT command. This can happen when the CONT command is given at

Error Message	*Cause*
	the END of the program. This could have also resulted because the program was never RUN, the program included an error, or a line has been edited.
DN or DEVICE NOT PRESENT	The computer has been commanded to OPEN, CLOSE, PRINT, or INPUT (CNP and GET on some computers) and the device required was not present. Coordinate the device with the correct number and continue.
DS	The computer has a direct statement in the data file. This could be caused if a program were loaded with no line numbers. Correct by assigning numbers.
/0 or DIVISION BY ZERO	This error results when the computer is commanded to divide a number by 0. Being impossible, the computer produces the error message.
EXTRA IGNORED	The computer received too many items of data in response to an input statement. Only the appropriate number and first in order will be accepted.
FM or NOT INPUT FILE or NOT OUTPUT FILE	The computer has been commanded to (1) INPUT data from a file OPEN for OUTPUT, or (2) PRINT data from a file that has been identified specifically for INPUT only.
FILE NOT FOUND	The computer was unable to find a file from tape and arrived at the END OF TAPE marker.
FILE OPEN or AO	The computer was commanded to open a file with a number on a file that is already open. If a proper number was being used, move to the next step. If an improper number was being used, correct number and command again.

Error Message	**Cause**
FORMULA TOO COMPLEX or ST	The computer has been commanded to complete a string formula that is too complex. The error can be resolved by breaking the task into smaller steps.
IO	The computer is attempting to execute the CLOAD command from a bad tape.
ILLEGAL DIRECT or ID	The computer was given an INPUT command in a direct mode. The INPUT statement can only be used during the program.
ILLEGAL QUANTITY or FC	The computer has been commanded to use a number to execute a function or statement that is out of the allowable range of the program or the computer. With a limit of 255 on sound, a command of SOUND 280 will produce this error. With a limit of 8, a command of CLD10 will produce this error.
LS or STRING TOO LONG	A string is limited to up to 225 characters.
LOAD	The computer has a problem with the program being loaded from the tape.
NF or NEXT WITHOUT FOR	The computer has been given a NEXT command without the correct corresponding FOR statement. The error is also sometimes caused by incorrect nesting loop.
NO or FILE NOT OPEN	The computer is to execute a CLOSE, CMD, PRINT, INPUT, or GET command and the file is not OPEN. The file first must be OPENed.
OV or OVERFLOW	The computer was commanded to handle a number that was larger than the computer's capacity allows. Reconstruct the program to allow for dealing with a smaller number.
OUT OF DATA or OD	The computer was given a READ command and there are no additional DATA to be READ in the DATA file. A DATA statement may have been

Error Message	***Cause***
	omitted from the program or more DATA were requested than had been stored. Either would produce this error.
OUT OF MEMORY or OM	This occurs when the computer is OUT OF MEMORY. All the available memory space has been used or reserved. Too many GOSUBs or FOR loops can contribute to the OUT OF MEMORY message.
REDIM'D ARRAY or DD	The computer has been commanded to DIMension an array that had already been DIMensioned. The program cannot have a DIM A 10 and a DIM A 20. Some machines will produce a REDIM'D ARRAY error if a variable is used before the array of DIM'd in the program. In this case the computer executes the DIM operation automatically and sets the number of elements on the array at 10. A DIM added at this point will produce an error.
REDO FROM START	Character data were submitted during the INPUT statement while numeric data were expected. Retype correct entry. Program will continue.
RETURN WITHOUT GOSUB or RG	The computer encountered a RETURN command and had not previously received a GOSUB command. Check program for inclusion of GOSUB or exclusion of the RETURN command.
SN or SYNTAX	The computer is unable to recognize the command due to misspelled word or words in the command, incorrect punctuation, addition of or missing parenthesis, or an incorrect character.
TYPE MISMATCH or TM	The computer has been commanded to assign numeric data to a string variable C$=4 or string data to a numeric variable C="DATA".

Error Message	***Cause***
UL or UNDEF'D STATEMENT	The computer was commanded to GOTO or GOSUB or in some cases RUN a line number that is nonexistent. These may be an incorrect or omitted line number or a typographical error in the number attached to the GOTO or GOSUB command. Each would produce this error.
VERIFY	The computer is unable to verify the program on the tape or disk with the program in the memory. Before shutting off the machine, SAVE again and VERIFY.

APPENDIX F

Comparison of BASIC Language for Three Computer Models: Apple, Commodore, TRS-80

Table AF-1
Comparison of BASIC Commands for Three Models

VIC-20	APPLE	TRS-80	PURPOSE
LOAD	LOAD	CLOAD	Loads the first program from cassette tape.
CONT	CONT	CONT	Continues executing a program after pressing BREAK or using STOP.
SAVE	SAVE	CSAVE	Saves a program on cassette tape.
DIM	DIM NAMES$	DIM	Reserves space in memory for the arrays you specify.
END	END	END	Ends your program.
For . . . TO STEP/NEXT	NEXT and For . . . TO STEP/NEXT	For . . . To STEP/NEXT	Creates a loop in your program which the computer must repeat from the first number to the last number you specify.
GOSUB	GOSUB	GOSUB	Sends the computer to the subroutine beginning at the line number you specify.

Table AF-1 *(Continued)*

VIC-20	APPLE	TRS-80	PURPOSE
GOTO	GOTO	GOTO	Sends the computer to the line number you specify.
If . . . Then	If . . . Then	If Then . . . Else	Tests the relationship.
INPUT	INPUT	INPUT	Causes the computer to stop and await input from the device you specify.
INT	INT	INT	Converts a number to an integer.
LEFT$	LEFT$	LEFT$	Returns the left portion of a string.
LEN	LEN	LEN	Returns the length of a string.
LIST	LIST	LIST	Lists the entire program or the lines in the program you specify.
MID$	MID$	MID$	Returns a substring within a string.
NEW	NEW	NEW	Erases everything in memory.
PRINT	PRINT	PRINT	Prints the message you specify on the device you specify.
REM	REM	REM	Allows you to insert a comment in your program.
RETURN	RETURN	RETURN	Returns the computer from the subroutine to the BASIC word following GOSUB.
RUN	RUN	RUN	Executes a program.
STR$	STR$	STR$	Converts a number to a string.
TAB	TAB	TAB	TABs to the position you specify.
VAL	VAR	VAL	Converts a string to a number.

Table AF-2
Comparison of BASIC Commands for the VIC-20 and TRS-80

VIC-20	TRS-80	PURPOSE
ABS	ABS	Computes the absolute value of a number
ASC	ASC	Converts the first character in a string to its ASCII code.
CHR$	CHR$	Converts an ASCII code to the character it represents.
CLR	CLS	Clears the screen to green or to the color code you specify.
DATA	DATA	Stores data in your program. Use READ to assign these data to variables.
ON . . . GOSUB	ON . . . GOSUB	Sends the computer to one of the subroutines you specify.
ON . . . GOTO	ON . . . GOTO	Sends the computer to one of line numbers you specify.

Table AF-2 (Continued)

VIC-20	TRS-80	PURPOSE
OPEN	OPEN	Opens communication to a device for inputting (I) or outputting (O) data.
PEEK	PEEK	Returns the contents in the memory location you specify.
POKE	POKE	Puts a value in the memory location you specify.
READ	READ	Reads the next item in the DATA line and assigns it to the variable you specify.
RESTORE	RESTORE	Sets the computer's pointer back to the first item on the DATA lines.
SGN	SGN	Tells the sign of a number.
SIN	SIN	Returns the sine in radians.
USR	USR	Calls a machine language subroutine whose address is stored at 275–276.
CLOSE	CLOSE	Closes a file by closing communication to the device you specify.
STOP	STOP	Makes the computer stop executing the program.

Table AF-3
Comparison of BASIC Commands for the Apple and TRS-80

APPLE	TRS-80	PURPOSE
CLEAR	CLEAR	Reserves space in the computer's memory for working with strings.
RIGHT$	RIGHT$	Returns the right portion of the string you specify beginning at the position you specify.
RND	RND	Returns a random integer between 1 and the number you specify.

Table AF-4
Summary of BASIC Commands for the Commodore VIC-20

COMMODORE VIC-20	PURPOSE
AND, OR, NOT	These are used most often to join multiple formulas in IF . . . THEN statements.
VERIFY	This command causes the VIC to check the program on tape or disk against the one in memory.

Table AF-4 (Continued)

COMMODORE VIC-20	PURPOSE
CMD	CMD sends the output that normally would go to the screen (i.e., PRINT statements, LISTS, but not POKE into the screen) to another device instead.
DEF FN (define function)	This command allows you to define a complex calculation as a function with a short name.
INPUT#	This works like INPUT, but takes the data from a previously OPENed file or device.
LET	The word LET itself is hardly ever used in programs since it is optional, but the statement is the heart of all BASIC programs.
NEXT	The NEXT statement is always used in conjunction with the FOR statement.
PRINT	There are a few differences between this statement and the PRINT.
STOP	This statement will halt the program.
SYS	The word SYS is followed by a decimal number or numeric variable in the range 0–65535.
WAIT	The WAIT statement is used to halt the program until the the contents of a location in memory change in a specific way.
ATN(x) (arctangent)	Returns the angle, measured in radians, whose tangent is X.
COS(x) (cosine)	Returns the value of the cosine of X, where X is an angle measured in radians.
EXP(x)	Returns the value of the mathematical constant e (2.71827183) raised to the power of X.
FNXX(x)	Returns the value of the user-defined function XX created in a DEF FNXX statement.
LOG(x) (logarithm)	This will return the natural log of X.
SQR(x) (square root)	This function will return the square root of X, where X is a positive number or 0.
TAN(x) (tangent)	The result will be the tangent of X, where X is an angle in radians.
FRE(x)	This function returns the number of unused bytes available in memory, regardless of the value of X.
POS(x)	This function returns the number of the column (0–21) at which the next PRINT statement will begin on the screen.
SPC(x)	This is used in the PRINT statement to skip X spaces forward.

Table AF-5
Summary of BASIC Commands for the TRS-80

TRS-80	PURPOSE
EO7	Checks to see if you have reached the end of the data in a file.
EXEC	Transfers control to a machine-language program at the address you specify.
INKEY$	Strobes the keyboard and returns the key or non-key being pressed.

JOYSTK	Returns the horizontal or vertical coordinate of the left or right joystick.
	    0 horizontal, right joystick
	    1 vertical, right joystick
	    2 horizontal, left joystick
	    3 vertical, left joystick

LLIST	Lists the entire program, or the lines you specify, on the printer.
MEM	Tells you how much space the computer has remaining in memory.
MOTOR	Turns the cassette ON or OFF.
POINT	Tells whether a dot at the horizontal and vertical location you specify is lit up.
PRINT @	Prints your message at the screen position you specify.
RESET	Erases the dot SET on the screen location you specify.
SET	Sets a dot at the screen location you specify, using the color you specify.
SKIPF	Skips to the end of the next program on cassette tape or to the end of the program you specify.
SOUND	Sounds the tone you specify for the duration you specify.
CLOADM	Loads a machine-language program from cassette tape.
AUDIO	Connects or disconnects the sound coming from your tape recorder to your TV.
CLOSE	Closes a file by closing communication to the device you specify.

Table AF-6
Summary of BASIC Commands for the Apple

APPLE	PURPOSE
ARROWKEYS	The keys marked with right- and left-pointing arrows are used to edit Applesoft programs.
CALL	Causes the asterisk prompt to appear indicating that the Apple is now responding to its native language called machine language.
CATALOG	Displays on the screen a list of all the files on the diskette in the specified or default drive.
COLOR	Sets the color for plotting in low-resolution graphics mode.
CTRL	Can be used to interrupt a RUNning program or a LISTing.
DEL	Removes the specified range of lines from the program.
ESCI, ESCJ, ESCK, ESCM	The escape key may be used in conjunction with the letter keys I or J or K or M to move the cursor without affecting the characters moved over by the cursor.
FLASH	Sets the video mode to "flashing," so the output from the computer is alternatively shown on the TV screen in white characters on black and then reversed to black characters on a white background.
HCOLOR	Sets high-resolution graphics color to the color specified by HCOLOR.
HGR	Only available in the firmware version of Applesoft.
HLIN AT	Used to draw horizontal lines in low-resolution graphics mode using the color most recently specified by COLOR.
HPLOT	Plots dots and lines in high-resolution graphics mode using the most recently specified value of HCOLOR.
HTAB	Moves the cursor either left or right to the specified column (1 through 40) on the screen.
INVERSE	Sets the video mode so that the computer's output prints as black letters on a white background.
LEFT ARROW	See ARROWKEYS.
NOTRACE	Turns off the TRACE mode.
NORMAL	Sets the video mode to the usual white letters on a black background for both input and output.
PDL	Returns the current value, a number from 0 through 225, of the indicated game control paddle.
PLOT	In low-resolution graphics mode, places a dot at the specified location.
COREX	To be printed.
REPT	If you hold down the repeat key, labeled REPT, while pressing any character key, the character will be repeated.

Table AF-6 *(Continued)*

APPLE	PURPOSE
RIGHT ARROW	See ARROWKEYS.
SAVE ADDRESSES	SAVEs the file currently in memory.
TEXT	Sets the screen to the usual nongraphics text mode, with 40 characters per line and 24 lines.
TRACE	Causes the line number of each statement to be displayed on the screen as it is executed.
VLIN	In low-resolution graphics mode, draws a vertical line in the color indicated by the most recent COLOR statement.
VTAB	Moves the cursor to the line on the screen specified by the argument.

APPENDIX G

Solutions to Self-Test Examples

Chapter 9

1 PRINT (12000 + 16000 + 11000 + 18500)/4
Result should be 14,375

2 PRINT "ONE TON OF FERTILIZER WHICH IS 33% NITROGEN
CONTAINS" .33 * 2000 "LBS OF NITROGEN"
Result: ONE TON OF FERTILIZER WHICH IS 33% NITROGEN
CONTAINS 660 LBS OF NITROGEN

Chapter 10

1 Soybean table: program and result

Program

```
10 PRINT "TOTAL AMERICAN SOYBEAN PRODUCTION"
15 PRINT "IN MILLIONS OF BUSHELS"
```

```
20 PRINT "YR/ACRE","TOTAL BU"
30 PRINT "1930-13.0",13.0*.9
40 PRINT "1960-23.4",23.4*24
45 PRINT "1980-32.2",32.2*71
```

Result

TOTAL AMERICAN SOYBEAN PRODUCTION
IN MILLIONS OF BUSHELS

YR/ACRE	TOTAL BU
1930–13.0	11.7
1960–23.4	561.6
1980–32.2	2286.2

2 Daily weight gain calculation

Program

```
10 PRINT "STEER WEIGHT GAIN CALCULATION"
15 PRINT "ENTER THE STEER'S ID"
20 INPUT A$
30 PRINT "ENTER BEGINNING WEIGHT"
40 INPUT F
45 PRINT "ENTER MARKET WEIGHT"
50 INPUT H
55 PRINT "ENTER DAYS ON FEED"
58 INPUT J
60 PRINT "DAILY GAIN OF STEER, "A$" WAS"(H-F)/J"POUNDS."
```

Result

STEER WEGIHT GAIN CALCULATION
ENTER THE STEER'S ID
   (type in JOE-74)
ENTER BEGINNING WEIGHT
   (type in 300)
ENTER MARKET WEIGHT
   (type in 975)
ENTER DAYS ON FEED
   (type in 200)
DAILY GAIN OF STEER, JOE-74 WAS 3.375 POUNDS

On line 60 remember that if you want addition or subtraction to
be done before multiplication or division, use parentheses.

Chapter 11

The operator LOADs and SAVEs on cassette tape and diskettes the programs of this chapter.

Chapter 12

1

```
5 PRINT "MARKET HOG DAILY GAIN"
10 PRINT "ENTER ID?"
15 INPUT C$
20 PRINT "ENTER DAYS ON FEED"
25 INPUT A
30 PRINT "ENTER WEIGHT GAINED"
35 INPUT D
40 PRINT "DAILY WEIGHT GAIN FOR  -"C$"-WAS"D/A"POUNDS."
50 STOP
60 GOTO 10
```

RUN program 1 and enter animal ID, days on feed, and weight gained on feed information. Such as animal ID, Miss Pig, days of feed, 120, and weight gained, 200 pounds. The program will complete the calculation and report a BREAK IN 50.
ENTER and CONT to restart the program.

2 You should have deleted line 50 to change program 1. However, the program is now in a loop and you will have to use the BREAK feature in order to STOP the new program.

```
5 PRINT "MARKET HOG DAILY GAIN"
10 PRINT "ENTER ID?"
15 INPUT C$
20 PRINT "ENTER DAYS ON FEED"
25 INPUT A
30 PRINT "ENTER WEIGHT GAINED"
35 INPUT D
40 PRINT "DAILY WEIGHT GAIN FOR  -"C$"-WAS"D/A"POUNDS."
60 GOTO 10
```

Chapter 13

1 Daily weight gain calculation

Program

```
10 PRINT "STEER WEIGHT GAIN CALCULATION"
15 PRINT "ENTER THE STEER ID"
20 INPUT A$
```

```
30 PRINT "ENTER BEGINNING WEIGHT"
40 INPUT F
45 PRINT "ENTER MARKET WEIGHT"
50 INPUT H
55 PRINT "ENTER DAYS ON FEED-MUST EXCEED 60"
60 INPUT J
65 IF J<60 THEN PRINT "MUST EXCEED 60 DAYS":GOTO 55
70 PRINT "DAILY GAIN OF STEER, "A$" WAS"(H-F)/J"POUNDS."
```

Result

STEER WEIGHT GAIN CALCULATION
ENTER THE STEER ID
   (type in JOE-74)
ENTER BEGINNING WEIGHT
   (type in 300)
ENTER MARKET WEIGHT
   (type in 975)
ENTER DAYS ON FEED - MUST EXCEED 60
   (type in 50 or more)
MUST EXCEED 60 DAYS
ENTER DAYS ON FEED - MUST EXCEED 60
   (type in 200)
DAILY GAIN OF STEER, JOE-74 WAS 3.375 POUNDS.

Chapter 14

```
10 PRINT "DETERMINE FIELD SIZE"
20 PRINT "CALCULATING THE NUMBER OF ACRES IN A RECTANGULAR FIELD."
30 PRINT "HOW LONG (IN FEET) IS THE FIELD?"
35 GOSUB 100
40 INPUT A
50 PRINT "HOW WIDE (IN FEET) IS THE FIELD?"
55 GOSUB 100
60 INPUT B
70 C=(A*B)/43560
80 PRINT "THE FIELD CONTAINS"C"ACRES."
90 END
100 PRINT "TYPE IN THE NUMBER AND PRESS ENTER TO CONTINUE."
110 RETURN
```

Chapter 15

1 Monthly Farm Feed and Supply Store Business

```
5 CLS
10 PRINT "FARM FEED AND SUPPLY STORE BUSINESS"
25 PRINT "ENTER SALESPERSON BASE MONTHLY SALARY"
30 INPUT A
35 PRINT "ENTER SALESPERSON COMMISSION RATE"
```

```
40 INPUT B
45 PRINT "JANITOR COST"
50 INPUT C
55 PRINT "ENTER GENERAL HELPER COST"
60 INPUT D
65 PRINT "ENTER FEED COST PER TON"
70 INPUT E
75 PRINT "ENTER FEED TONS SOLD PER MONTH"
80 INPUT F
85 PRINT "ENTER APPLIANCES EXPENSE PER MONTH"
90 INPUT G
95 PRINT "ELECTRICITY BILL"
100 INPUT H
105 PRINT "HEAT AND COOLING BILL"
110 INPUT I
115 PRINT "FEED SALE PRICE PER TON"
120 INPUT J
125 PRINT "TONS OF FEED SOLD"
130 INPUT K
135 PRINT "ENTER APPLIANCE SALES PER MONTH"
140 INPUT L
145 CLS
150 LET M=K*J
152 LET N=M+L
154 LET O=A+B+C+D
155 LET Q=H+I
156 LET P=E*F+L
160 PRINT "LABOR EXPENSE $"O
162 PRINT "MATERIALS SOLD EXPENSE $"P
165 PRINT "FIXED AND BUILDING EXPENSE $"Q
170 PRINT "FEED INCOME $"M
175 PRINT "APPLIANCES INCOME $"L
180 PRINT "TOTAL STORE EXPENSES $"P
185 PRINT "TOTAL STORE INCOME $"N
190 IF N<P THEN 230
195 PRINT "STORE PROFIT WAS $"N-P
200 END
230 PRINT "STORE LOSS WAS $"P-N
235 END
```

With the given figures the correct answer are as follows:

Labor expense	$ 2,556.40
Materials sold expense	17,000.00
Fixed & building expense	275.00
Feed income	17,820.00
Applicances income	5,000.00
Total expenses	17,000.00
Store total income	22,820,00
Profit	5,320.00

2 Make the following changes in the first program. Start with line 200, remove the END statement, and replace with:

```
5 CLS
10 PRINT "FARM FEED AND SUPPLY STORE BUSINESS"
25 PRINT "ENTER SALESPERSON BASE MONTHLY SALARY"
30 INPUT A
35 PRINT "ENTER SALESPERSON COMMISSION RATE"
40 INPUT B
45 PRINT "JANITOR COST"
50 INPUT C
55 PRINT "ENTER GENERAL HELPER COST"
60 INPUT D
65 PRINT "ENTER FEED COST PER TON"
70 INPUT E
75 PRINT "ENTER FEED TONS SOLD PER MONTH"
80 INPUT F
85 PRINT "ENTER APPLIANCES EXPENSE PER MONTH"
90 INPUT G
95 PRINT "ELECTRICITY BILL"
100 INPUT H
105 PRINT "HEAT AND COOLING BILL"
110 INPUT I
115 PRINT "FEED SALE PRICE PER TON"
120 INPUT J
125 PRINT "TONS OF FEED SOLD"
130 INPUT K
135 PRINT "ENTER APPLIANCE SALES PER MONTH"
140 INPUT L
145 CLS
150 LET M=K*J
152 LET N=M+L
154 LET O=A+B+C+D
155 Q=H+I
156 P=E*F+L
160 PRINT "LABOR EXPENSE $"O
162 PRINT "MATERIALS SOLD EXPENSE $"P
165 PRINT "FIXED AND BUILDING EXPENSE $"Q
170 PRINT "FEED INCOME $"M
175 PRINT "APPLIANCES INCOME $"L
180 PRINT "TOTAL STORE EXPENSES $"P
185 PRINT "TOTAL STORE INCOME $"N
190 IF N<P THEN 230
195 PRINT "STORE PROFIT WAS $"N-P
200 PRINT "IF YOU WANT AN ANNUAL STATEMENT ENTER YES: IF NOT ENTER NO"
205 INPUT A$
210 IF A$="YES" THEN 300
230 PRINT "STORE LOSS WAS $"P-N
235 PRINT "IF YOU WANT AN ANNUAL STATEMENT ENTER YES: IF NOT ENTER NO"
240 INPUT A$
250 IF A$="YES" THEN 290
260 END
290 CLS
300 PRINT "ANNUAL EXPENSES ARE"
305 PRINT "LABOR $"12*O
310 PRINT "MATERIALS $"12*P
315 PRINT "FIXED AND BUILDINGS $"12*Q
335 PRINT "FEED INCOME IS $"M*12
340 PRINT "APPLIANCE INCOME IS $"L*12
360 PRINT "ANNUAL INCOME IS $"12*N
370 PRINT "ANNUAL EXPENSES IS $"12*P
375 IF P>N THEN 410
380 PRINT "ANNUAL PROFIT IS $"12*(N-P)
390 END
410 PRINT "ANNUAL LOSS IS $"12*(P-N)
```

Chapter 16

Program I

Line 10: The first set of question marks is omitted.

Line 30: A string variable is used where a numerical variable is needed.

Line 80: A string variable cannot be used in a formula calculation.

Line 95: The variable C cannot be enclosed by quotation marks.

Line 120: This GOSUB command is not necessary.

Line 170: This END is outside the loop and serves no purpose.

Corrected Program I

```
10 PRINT "CALCULATING THE NUMBER OF ACRES IN A FIELD."
20 PRINT "HOW LONG (FEET) IS THE FIELD?"
25 GOSUB 150
30 INPUT A
50 PRINT "HOW WIDE (FEET) IS THE FIELD?"
55 GOSUB 150
60 INPUT B
80 C=(A*B)/43560
90 PRINT "THE FIELD CONTAINS " C "ACRES"
95 IF C >100 THEN PRINT C " ACRES IS A LARGE FIELD."
100 END
150 PRINT "TYPE IN THE NUMBER AND PRESS ENTER TO CONTINUE"
160 RETURN
```

Program II

PRINT	Line 10:	The quotation marks following the word TEMPERATURE should be deleted.
INPUT	Line 20:	The input variable should be a numerical variable.
IF-THEN	Line 30:	The numerical variable A should not be enclosed in quotation marks.
GOTO	Line 30:	The end of line 30 should read: GOTO 10

| GOSUB | Line 60: GOSUB places the program into a subroutine and should read GOSUB 2000. |
| REM | Line 70: REM FRED WAS HERE is irrelevant and should be deleted. |

Corrected Program II

```
5 PRINT "CORN PLANTING SOIL TEMPERATURES"
10 PRINT "WHAT TEMPERATURE IS NEEDED FOR CORN SEED GERMINATION?"
20 INPUT A
30 IF A <>55 THEN PRINT "WRONG ANSWER, TRY AGAIN":GOTO 10
40 PRINT "YOU ARE CORRECT."
50 PRINT "SOIL TEMPERATURES BELOW 55 CAN CAUSE POOR GERMINATION."
60 GOSUB 2000
150 END
2000 FOR X = 1 TO 1000:NEXT
2010 PRINT "GOOD ANSWER!"
2100 RETURN
```

Program III

Line 50:	Must use a string variable.
Line 60:	Quotation marks must follow the PRINT command.
Line 130:	The variable must be a string variable (B$).
Line 160:	Because the INPUT variable will be used in a formula calculation, a numerical variable must be used.
Line 230:	The program will not make sense unless the GOTO is to line 330.

Corrected Program III

```
10 PRINT "SPRAYING"
20 PRINT "THIS PROGRAM CAN HELP YOU CALCULATE TOTAL SPRAY VOLUME PER ACRE"
30 PRINT "FOR A BROADCAST SPRAYER."
40 PRINT "PRESS <RETURN> TO CONTINUE..."
50 INPUT A$
60 PRINT "SPRAY A TEST STRIP 660 FEET LONG AND MEASURE WATER USAGE."
80 PRINT "YOU WILL NEED TO KNOW THE"
90 PRINT "WIDTH <FEET> OF YOUR SPRAYER."
100 PRINT "DO YOU HAVE THE NEEDED INFORMATION?"
110 PRINT "ENTER Y FOR YES OR N FOR NO <AND PRESS RETURN>"
120 INPUT B$
130 IF B$ = "N" THEN 300
140 PRINT "HOW WIDE A SWATH DOES YOUR SPRAYER MAKE <FEET>?"
150 GOSUB 350
160 INPUT A
170 PRINT "HOW MUCH WATER DID YOU USE IN THE TEST STRIP <GALLONS>?"
180 GOSUB 350
190 INPUT B
```

```
200 LET C = (B/A)*66
210 PRINT "AT THE PRESENT CALIBRATION -- YOUR SPRAYER"
220 PRINT "DELIVERS "C" GALLONS OF SPRAY MATERIAL (VOLUME) PER ACRE."
230 GOTO 330
300 PRINT "THEN YOU SHOULD LEAVE NOW TO GET THAT INFORMATION."
310 PRINT "THE PROGRAM HAS ENDED FOR NOW."
320 PRINT "YOU CAN START AT THE BEGINNING WHEN YOU RETURN."
330 PRINT "  --THE END--  "
340 END
350 PRINT "ENTER NUMBER AND PRESS (RETURN)"
360 RETURN
```

Chapter 17

```
10 PRINT "STEER WEIGHT GAIN CALCULATION"
12 FOR X = 1 TO 1500:NEXT
15 PRINT "ENTER THE STEER ID"
20 INPUT A$
30 PRINT "ENTER BEGINNING WEIGHT"
40 INPUT F
45 PRINT "ENTER MARKET WEIGHT"
50 INPUT H
55 PRINT "ENTER DAYS ON FEED - MUST EXCEED 60"
60 INPUT J
65 IF J < 60 THEN PRINT "MUST EXCEED 60 DAYS":GOTO 55
70 PRINT "DAILY GAIN OF STEER, "A$" WAS "(H-F)/J" POUNDS."
```

Result: The program will run as it did in Chapter 13 except it will pause at line 12 before going to line 15.

Chapter 18

1 75
   85
   95
   99

2 Score 1   Score 2
    75   85
    95   99

3

```
10 DATA FRED,99,JOE,88,JAY,95
20 DATA TOM,96,JIM,98,BOB,85
30 PRINT "NAME","SCORE"
40 FOR T = 1 TO 2
```

```
50 READ A$,A,B$,B,C$,C
60 PRINT A$,A,B$,B,C$,C
70 NEXT
```

Results

NAME	SCORE
FRED	99
JOE	88
JAY	95
TOM	96
JIM	98
BOB	85

Chapter 19

```
10 DATA JONES,511,4.75
20 DATA SMITH,611,5.10
30 DATA BROWN,711,9.00
70 PRINT "WHICH OF THE FOLLOWING ITEMS DO YOU WANT?"
75 RESTORE
80 PRINT "1.   WORKERS NAMES"
85 PRINT "2.   NAMES AND ID NUMBERS"
90 PRINT "3.   NAMES, ID'S AND SALARY"
95 PRINT "4.   ENTER 4 TO END PROGRAM"
100 INPUT A
110 IF A = 1 THEN 1000
120 IF A = 2 THEN 2000
130 IF A = 3 THEN 3000
140 IF A = 4 THEN END
150 FOR T = 1 TO 500:NEXT
1000 CLS
1010 PRINT "COWBOY FARM WORKERS"
1020 PRINT "NAMES-"
1022 FOR X = 1 TO 3
1024 READ A$,B$,C$
1025 PRINT A$
1028 NEXT
1030 FOR T = 1 TO 500:NEXT
1035 CLS
1040 GOTO 70
2000 CLS
2010 PRINT "COWBOY FARM WORKERS"
2020 PRINT "-NAMES--ID NO.-"
2030 FOR X = 1 TO 3
2040 READ A$,B$,C$
2050 PRINT A$"----"B$
2060 NEXT
```

```
2070 FOR T = 1 TO 500:NEXT
2075 CLS
2080 GOTO 70
3000 CLS
3010 PRINT "COWBOY FARM WORKERS"
3020 PRINT "-NAMES--ID NO.--HR$-"
3030 FOR X = 1 TO 3
3040 READ A$,B$,C$
3050 PRINT A$"----"B$"----"C$
3060 NEXT
3070 FOR T = 1 TO 500:NEXT
3075 CLS
3080 GOTO 70
```

Chapter 20

1

```
10 PRINT "MILK PRODUCTION"
20 DATA 6,8,7,5,4,5,4
30 DATA 18000,20000,17000,15000,16000,21000,19000
40 DIM A(7),B(7)
50 PRINT "COW-";"AGE-";"PRODUCTION"
90 FOR X = 1 TO 7
100 READ A(X)
110 NEXT
120 FOR X = 1 TO 7
130 READ B(X)
140 NEXT
144 X=0
148 X=X+1
149 IF X = 8 THEN END
150 PRINT X;A(X);B(X)
160 GOTO 148
```

2

```
10 DIM A$(12)
20 DATA HACKSAW,HACKSAW BLADES,BENCH RULE,METAL SNIPS,FILE,COLD CHISEL
30 DATA CENTER PUNCH,PLIERS,SCRATCH AWL, COMB SQUARE,B.P. HAMMER,WOODEN MALLET
35 PRINT "TOOLS IN STOCK"
40 FOR X = 1 TO 12
50 READ A$(X)
60 PRINT X;A$(X)
70 NEXT
```

Chapter 21

1

```
10 PRINT TAB(12) "WELCOME"
20 PRINT TAB(6) "AGRICULTURAL SOCIETY"
30 PRINT TAB(13) "1990"
```

Chapter 22

```
10 PRINT "B & I EQUIPMENT SALES"
20 PRINT "RECORD OF TRACTORS SOLD DURING LAST FISCAL YEAR"
30 DATA 125,228,245,247,252,301,306,308,310,311
50 DATA 12000,28000,35000,14000,12500,60000,35000,45000,15000,15500
70 DATA 8000,20000,32000,10000,10300,58000,33000,42000,11000,13500
90 DIM A(10),B(10),C(10),D(10)
100 FOR X = 1 TO 10
110 READ A(X)
120 NEXT
130 FOR X = 1 TO 10
140 READ B(X)
150 NEXT
160 FOR X = 1 TO 10
170 READ C(X)
180 NEXT
190 PRINT "EQUIP-PRICE-COST-PROFIT"
200 X=0
210 X=X+1
220 IF X = 11 THEN 270
230 D(X)=B(X)-C(X)
240 PRINT A(X);B(X);C(X);D(X)
245 FOR T = 1 TO 500:NEXT
250 GOTO 210
270 PRINT "B & I PURCHASE EQUIPMENT FROM THREE SOURCES."
271 FOR T=1 TO 2000:NEXT T:CLS
272 PRINT "WOULD YOU LIKE TO KNOW WHERE TO PURCHASE SPECIFIC EQUIPMENT";
275 INPUT A$
277 IF A$<>"YES" THEN 1000
278 PRINT "PRESS 1,2, OR 3 TO DETERMINE EQUIPMENT SOURCE BY EQUIPMENT#."
285 PRINT TAB(5)"(1)EQUIP# 125,228,245"
290 PRINT TAB(5)"(2)EQUIP# 247,252,301"
295 PRINT TAB(5)"(3)EQUIP# 306,308,310,311"
300 PRINT TAB(1)"(ENTER '4' TO END THIS PROGRAM)"
305 INPUT R
307 IF R = 4 THEN 1000
308 ON R GOSUB 400,500,600
310 GOSUB 700
315 CLS
320 GOTO 278
400 PRINT"EQUIPMENT#"
410 PRINT TAB(8)"125"
420 PRINT TAB(8)"228"
430 PRINT TAB(8)"245"
460 PRINT TAB(12)"FROM"
470 PRINT TAB(5)"T.C. EQUIPMENT"
480 PRINT TAB(5)"2500 5TH ST."
490 PRINT TAB(5)"ROCKFORT, OH 61522"
494 GOSUB 700
495 CLS
496 GOTO 278
500 PRINT "EQUIPMENT#"
510 PRINT TAB(8)"247"
520 PRINT TAB(8)"252"
530 PRINT TAB(8)"301"
560 PRINT TAB(12)"FROM"
570 PRINT TAB(5)"BOB WHITE WHOLESALE"
580 PRINT TAB(5)"354TH ST."
590 PRINT TAB(5)"CLEVELAND, IN 32141"
595 GOSUB 700
596 GOTO 278
600 PRINT "EQUIPMENT#"
610 PRINT TAB(8)"306"
620 PRINT TAB(8)"308"
630 PRINT TAB(8)"310"
640 PRINT TAB(8)"311"
660 PRINT TAB(12)"FROM"
670 PRINT TAB(5)"TRACTOR SUPPLY INC."
680 PRINT TAB(5)"1385 N. CLAY ST."
690 PRINT TAB(5)"TAMPA, GA 23566"
```

```
695 GOSUB 700
696 CLS
698 GOTO 278
700 FOR T=1 TO 1500:NEXT T
710 CLS
720 RETURN
1000 PRINT "          ----THE END----"
1010 END
```

Chapter 23

1 Feed Letters

2 Swine Production

1 Dairy Example

COORDINATE ENTRIES

	A	B	C	D	E
1	NAME	DAY PROD	AGE	ACT PROD	ADJ PROD
2	ADA	40	4	305 * B2	D2 * 1.08
3	BOSSY	45	3	305 * B3	D3 * 1.18
4	GEORGE	42	3	305 * B4	D4 * 1.18
5	HANK	56	6	305 * B5	D5

COORDINATE DISPLAY

	A	B	C	D	E
1	NAME	DAY PROD	AGE	ACT PROD	ADJ PROD
2	ADA	40	4	12200	13176
3	BOSSY	45	3	13725	16195
4	GEORGE	42	3	12810	15115
5	HANK	56	6	17080	17080

2 Grain Storage Problem

COORDINATE ENTRIES

	A	B	C	D	E	F	G	H
1		Current	Jan 1	Feb 1	Mar 1	Apr 1	May 1	Jun 1
2	Bushels	30,000	replicate B2					
3	Fix Stor	900	replicate B3					
4	Var Stor	0	.02*B2	.02*B2+C4 (replicate formula C-G)				.02*F2+G4
5	Price	2.10	B5*1.05	(replicate formula with relative function)				
				G5*1.05				
6	Net		(B2*B5)−(B3+B4) replicate formulas with relative functions (H2*H5)−(H3+H4)					

COORDINATE DISPLAY

	A	B	C	D	E	F	G	H
		Current	Jan 1	Feb 1	Mar 1	Apr 1	May 1	Jun 1
2	Bushels	30,000	30,000	30,000	30,000	30,000	30,000	30,000
3	Fix Stor	900	900	900	900	900	900	900
4	Var Stor	0	600	1200	1800	2400	3000	3600
5	Price	2.10	2.205	2.31	2.43	2.55	2.68	2.81
6	Net	62100	64650	67357	70230	73276	76505	79926

Index